Homosexuality and the Family

Homosexuality and the Family

Frederick W. Bozett, RN, DNS
Editor

Homosexuality and the Family was simultaneously issued by The Haworth Press, Inc. under the same title, as a special issue of the *Journal of Homosexuality*, Volume 18, Numbers 1/2, 1989.

Harrington Park Press
New York • London

ISBN 0-918393-57-4

Published by

Harrington Park Press, Inc., 10 Alice Street, Binghamton, New York 13904-1580
EUROSPAN/Harrington, 3 Henrietta Street, London WC2E 8LU England

Harrington Park Press, Inc., is a subsidiary of The Haworth Press, Inc., 10 Alice Street, Binghamton, New York 13904-1580.

Homosexuality and the Family was originally published as *Journal of Homosexuality*, Volume 18, Numbers 1/2 1989.

Cover design by Marshall Andrews.

Library of Congress Cataloging-in-Publication Data

Homosexuality and the Family / Frederick W. Bozett, editor.
    p. cm.
    "Originally published as Journal of homosexuality, volume18, numbers 1/2 1989" — Verso of CIP t.p.
    Includes bibliographical references and index.
    ISBN 0-918393-57-4
    1. Gays — Family relationships. I. Bozett, Frederick W.
[HQ76.25.H6755   1989b]
306.7′66 — dc20
                       89-7524
                          CIP

CONTENTS

ALL HAWORTH BOOKS & JOURNALS
ARE PRINTED ON CERTIFIED
ACID-FREE PAPER

ABOUT THE EDITOR

Frederick W. Bozett, RN, DNS, is a professor in the graduate program, College of Nursing, University of Oklahoma. He is editor of *Gay and Lesbian Parents* (Praeger, 1987) and co-editor of *Dimensions of Fatherhood* (Sage, 1985). He has published extensively in the area of fatherhood and gay fathers. Dr. Bozett is currently undertaking a longitudinal study of custodial gay father families, as well as studies of gay father-child relationships and gay grandfathers.

Homosexuality and the Family

Preface

This collection concerns homosexuality in the family. To many, linking lesbians and gays with the word "family" is a contradiction in terms. Rev. Jerry Falwell, in a 1980 sermon, flatly declared "Homosexuals are antifamily." Evidence suggests, however, that lesbians and gays are as involved with family life as heterosexuals. The nine papers collected for this special collection are the beginnings of research into this area.

What are some of the forms that homosexuality in the family takes? First, there are traditional family structures where a member is homosexual: it can be a parent, a teenage sibling, or a grandparent. Second, there are voluntary aggregates that lesbians and gays call families: homosexual friendship networks, lesbian/gay couples, and homosexual communes. Although my data are limited to anecdotal accounts, several examples from my own circle illustrate these arrangements:

1. Three sets of lovers buy into a multiunit dwelling. Each couple has its own condominium, but they visit each other's homes so often that the building functions as a communal space.
2. A pair of gay couples rents a huge home together with more room than either couple could have afforded alone, and with plenty of space for joint entertaining.
3. A pair of lesbian couples lives separately in the city, but they buy a small country cottage together where all four of them spend their weekends.
4. Two gay friends, though never residing together or having sex together, phone each other every day, attend concerts, movies, dinner parties, bars, and the gym with each other. When one recently had surgery, the other took time off from work to help with his friend's convalescence.
5. Two gay lovers maintain separate residences over the nine

xi

years of their relationship asserting that cohabitation is not necessary for intimacy.

Raising children can be as much a purpose for lesbians and gays forming families as for heterosexuals:

1. Two lesbian mothers become lovers after leaving their husbands. The women rent a house, and together they coparent a combined family of seven children.
2. A divorced gay father and his lover double their household instantly when his two teenage daughters run away from their mother and say they want to live with dad and their new gay stepfather.
3. In 1986, Los Angeles County approved the placement of a foster child with a homosexual physician.
4. A lesbian couple have a child by artificial insemination. As a family they attract a host of satellites, singles, and other couples. The extended network of gay friends becomes the child's aunts and uncles.

Additionally, the above relationships may be open or closed, biological or adoptive, contractual or informal. They may be multigenerational, composed of commuter couples, or ex-lovers. These pairs, friendship circles, sister/brotherhoods, marriages, and communes comprise what lesbians and gays call "family."

These arrangements, however, are not trouble free. Lesbian and gay couples, just like their heterosexual counterparts, have conflicts about privacy, power, jealousy, intimacy, freedom, definitions of friendship (including sexual friendships), searching for a balance between "I" and "us." We struggle against a society that believes that because gay relationships statistically do not last as many years as nongay ones (though many, of course, do), they are less valid; that families that go unblessed by the church and the courts are not families. We also struggle against a homophobic society that instills self-hatred: a self-hatred that sometimes sabotages gay families from within as well as from without.

In spite of these difficulties, lesbians and gays continue to be involved in family life just as we have done for centuries. Indeed, the lifestyles described above are not so much a revolutionary but an evolutionary part of a long process of homosexuals defining and redefining ourselves.

This material prompts an interesting question: Given the history of gay involvement in the family, why has so little empirical research been accomplished? One reason may be that research on the family is a low status area in academia. Possibly this is because it is seen as "women's research." Research on gays' family involvement is ranked even lower because it carries the additional stigma of homosexuality. Thus, sexism and homophobia combine to devalue the area.

Another reason why investigators may avoid gay family research is stigma contamination: The soiled status of respondents rubs off on those who choose to study them. So great is this problem that many who are lesbian or gay and who do homosexual research keep two resumes, one which is conventional, and one which includes lesbian and gay publications. Others change titles so that the word "homosexual" is replaced by "variant" or some such euphemism. Although these strategies can be justified in the name of job survival in a hostile environment, there is the lingering suspicion that employing such passing strategies involves residual shame about lesbian/gay identity.

The most parsimonious explanation to account for the dearth of scholarship on lesbians and gays in the family is that nobody ever thought about it until recently. We have been overshadowed by society's heterosexual hegemony. Moves to counteract this have been made by the Association of Lesbian and Gay Psychologists, another form of gay family for those of us in the field.

The nine articles in this collection are arranged in a life-history sequence that moves from adolescence to adulthood. Though they offer no formal definitions, they show by example the scope of homosexuality in the family. Savin-Williams, employing questionnaire data from 317 homosexual youths, identified the salient variables affecting their self-esteem and disclosure to their parents. Robinson, Walters, and Skeen surveyed 402 parents of lesbians and gays and documented parental responses to (a) learning that their child is homosexual, and (b) their feelings about AIDS. DiLapi discussed the stigma surrounding lesbian mothers and the societal values that buttress this negative perception. Hays and Samuels, using questionnaire data from 21 wives of gay men, discussed the women's feelings and adjustments regarding their marriages. Bozett reviewed the research literature on gay fathers and compared studies of gay fathers with other groups such as lesbian mothers and nongay fathers. Huggins questioned 36 teenage children of lesbian and heterosexual mothers to determine if there were any differences in the adolescents' self-esteem. Bigner and Jacobsen, using questionnaire data from 33 gay fathers and 33 nongay fathers, assessed the relative importance of children in the respondents' lives, and compared differences in their parenting behaviors.

Regardless of the broad diversity of the articles, they share important characteristics. All but one have been funded out of the authors' pockets, a reality that necessarily limits their scope and makes their findings suggestive rather than definitive, a caution the authors acknowledge. Another similarity is that none of the authors is primarily concerned with providing descriptions of sexual settings or encounters, or of discussing etiology: goals that too long have been the preoccupation of researchers who give the impression that they are aloof and only "slumming" in our territories. These articles attempt to go further by clarifying some of the complex linkages between sexuality and other areas of family life.

Brian Miller, PhD
Psychotherapist, Private Practice
Los Angeles

Coming Out to Parents and Self-Esteem Among Gay and Lesbian Youths

Ritch C. Savin-Williams, PhD

Cornell University

SUMMARY. The significance of the parents for the coming out process and for the self-evaluation of 317 gay and lesbian youths between the ages of 14 and 23 years was assessed in the current study. Responses from a 10-page questionnaire are analyzed, and these findings are discussed in the context of sex differences for both adolescents and parents, the importance of the parents for the self-esteem of gay and lesbian youth, and limitations of the current investigation.

For many gay and lesbian youths, the most difficult decision to make after recognizing, and then accepting to some degree, their nontraditional sexual orientation is to reveal to their parents that they will not be fulfilling the heterosexual dreams of the parents. This appears intuitively obvious and, indeed, "coming out right" advice books strongly emphasize the critical importance of the parents in the coming out process. On the other hand, published theoretical models that describe the coming out process have largely

Dr. Savin-Williams is Professor of Social/Personality Development in the Department of Human Development at Cornell University.

The author expresses his appreciation to the undergraduate research assistants who collected many of the questionnaires and who were a delight to work with: Beth Burlingame, Andrea Butt, Jay Coburn, Richard Goldberg, and Rala Massey.

Correspondence and reprint requests may be addressed to Ritch C. Savin-Williams, Department of Human Development, Cornell University, Ithaca, NY 14853.

1

ignored the role that the parents have on this aspect of their child's development and the resulting self-evaluation that the gay or lesbian adolescent maintains. A companion paper (Savin-Williams, 1989) explored the relationship between the parents' reaction (or would react if they knew) to the knowledge of their son's or daughter's homosexuality and the youth's comfortableness being gay and his or her self-esteem level. The research reported here extends that investigation by examining (a) characteristics of the parents and the youth's relationship with them that influence the parents' knowledge of the sexual orientation of their son or daughter, and (b) how these in combination affect the youth's self-esteem.

The self-help, advice literature is quite explicit in highlighting the significance of the parents in the youth's coming out process and self-evaluation. Some gays and lesbians never come out to their parents, becoming, according to MacDonald (1983),

> half-members of the family unit: afraid and alienated, unable ever to be totally open and spontaneous, to trust or be trusted, to develop a fully socialized sense of self-affirmation. This sad stunting of human potential breeds stress for gay people and their families alike — stress characterized by secrecy, ignorance, helplessness, and distance. (p. 1)

These youths may respond by running away from home or by becoming involved in prostitution or other crimes because they are unable to cope with the obligatory deception, isolation, and alienation (Clark, 1977; Martin, 1982).

Gay teenagers have given first-person accounts of the emotional significance, and danger, of coming out to parents (Heron, 1983):

> Perhaps nothing is riskier than coming out to parents. I came out to my parents at the same time I came out to myself, but I wasn't prepared for their reaction. . . . "You can't be gay! You must be mistaken." They were so upset they sent me back to school and said, "Don't come back home until we say you can." Those were the most painful words I've ever heard. For a brief moment I considered suicide, but I had friends and ministers to turn to for support. I was not alone. (Rick, p. 97)

. . . I was given the conditions of my return: 1. Give up my lifestyle. 2. Like girls. 3. Give up all past friends. . . . Dad escorted me to the garage where I was harassed. "You fucking queer, you goddamn faggot . . . Sissy. . . . Do you actually have sex with your lover?" "I don't think it's any of your business." Grabbing my throat, Dad shouted, "It is my fucking business." (Jim, p. 43)

I also told my father. The one phrase that I'll remember is, "Your mother and I have no further reason to live. I don't know what the hell we have done to deserve the treatment we are getting. Terry, you were our only hope." (Terry, p. 73)

In books written to assist the gay or lesbian individual to develop in a healthy manner, there is a careful, considered approach to the issue of revealing one's sexual orientation to parents; one must balance the gains and losses because parents have the capacity and power to inflict ostracism, rejection, isolation, and even violence (Muchmore & Hanson, 1982; Silverstein, 1977). Generally, parents should not be told unless the youth has developed a relatively secure, positive view of homosexuality and has a good relationship with the parents (Silverstein, 1977).

Given the historical condemnation of homosexuality as sin, sickness, and crime, and the tendency for most parents to consider their children to be extensions of themselves, "It is not surprising that difficulty with parents is among the most significant problems in the lives of many homosexuals" (Weinberg, 1972, p. 92). For some, telling parents is the final exit out of the closet (Fairchild & Hayward, 1979). This last book, as well as others (Borhek, 1983; Clark, 1977; Silverstein, 1977), suggested strategies for parents to help them cope with the seemingly earth-shattering news of their child's homosexuality.

The most accurate generalization that can be made, however, is that the reaction of parents to the news appears "unpredictable" (Borhek, 1983), although most writers believe that a positive prior relationship with the parents is a good indicator for a healthy resolution (Borhek, 1983; Fairchild & Hayward, 1979; Silverstein, 1977; Weinberg, 1972). Elderly parents may have more difficulty accepting their child's homosexuality because of the social and political climate of their childrearing years (e.g., the McCarthy era) when homosexuality was viewed as an unspeakable, moral sin or a deep, psychological pathology (Borhek, 1983).

The advice literature is less in agreement on the effects that coming out to parents has on the self-evaluations of the gay or lesbian individual. If the consequences are affirming and supportive, then telling will enhance one's self-esteem:

> You may have a clearer sense of your identity and a new sense of freedom and self-respect because now you are not hiding your real self. . . . You may now be able to share joyfully and with a sense of well-being with the significant persons in your life because you have taken the positive step of being real with them. In other words, by risking coming out to your parents you have given yourself and them an opportunity to grow. (Borhek, 1983, p. 20)

In contrast to this high priority on the parent-child relationship for youth during the revelation process, the theoretical and empirical coming out literature largely ignores the issue (Cass, 1979, 1984; Dank, 1971; de Monteflores & Schultz, 1978; Lee, 1977; MacDonald, 1982; Myrick, 1974; Plummer, 1975; Schafer, 1977; Troiden, 1979, 1988; Weinberg, 1978). Troiden (1989) noted that an accepting family is one of several facilitating factors in the coming out process. Myrick (1974) unceremoniously included "out to family" with employer, future employer, male acquaintance, and best heterosexual friend in his measure of self-disclosure. Cass (1979) treated parents as just one aspect of a category that included peers, church group, and heterosexuals in general as a determining factor in whether the gay/lesbian individual will "pass" as a heterosexual or come out. Coleman (1982), however, noted the significance of telling parents, but the youth should first gauge if the parents will be accepting.

There is relatively little empirical research on the factors that determine whether the adolescent will reveal his or her homosexuality to the parents or on the effects that coming out to parents have on a youth's self-esteem. In general, gay and lesbian youth are more likely to come out to mothers than to fathers: 44% and 32%, respectively, in a West German sample of lesbians (Schafer, 1976), and 42% and 31% (males) and 49% and 37% (females) in a San Francisco Bay Area sample of white homosexual persons (Bell & Weinberg, 1978). In the former population of lesbians, 62% of the mothers and 43% of the fathers "accepted and understood." In the latter group, self-acceptance was highest among those adult gay men who were most likely to be out to their parents (functionals and close-coupleds) and lowest among those least likely to be out to parents (dysfunctionals and asexuals). No such trend was evident among the women.

In the current sample of youths, a lesbian felt most comfortable with her sexual orientation if she also reported that her parents accepted, or would accept if they knew, her sexual orientation; their perceived acceptance did not, however, predict her level of self-esteem (Savin-Williams, 1989). Among males, parental acceptance was related to a youth feeling comfortable being gay if he also reported that the parents were important to his sense of self-worth; males comfortable with their sexual orientation had the highest level of self-esteem.

Thus, based on this earlier analysis of the data and the gay advice literature, there is reason to believe that the parents are a significant factor in the developing sense of sexual identity for gay and lesbian youth, especially in terms of comfortableness and acceptance of one's sexual orientation and in one's general self-evaluation (at least among males). The theoretical coming out literature, however, appears to contradict these assertions by essentially ignoring the role of the parents in the coming out process. The research reported here bridges these two literatures by proposing that the following variables increase the probability that the parents know the sexual orientation of their child: (a) the youth reports satisfaction and contact with the parent, (b) the parents are married rather than separated or divorced, and (c) the parents are young rather than old.

In addition, these variables, and the fact that the parent knows, should predict a high level of self-esteem for the adolescent. Because of the possibility that these relationships are dependent on the sex of the adolescent or the parent, or both, all analyses in this study were conducted separately for gay males and lesbians and for fathers and mothers. To explore whether the findings are specific to particular populations of gays and lesbians, the analyses were further subdivided for each age, community, occupational status, and sexual orientation grouping of the youths.

METHODS

The Youths

The age range of the 317 participating youths was 14 to 23 years. The 214 gay males and 103 lesbians were for the most part (81%) in high school or college during data collection; 19% had 12 or fewer years of education. Although most (91%) were Caucasian, the youths were diverse in religious heritage: one third Catholic, one third Protestant, and one third other (none, Jewish, Eastern). The youths grew up in homes from a variety of community sizes and occupational statuses: rural or small towns (44%), medium-sized towns (27%), small cities (12%), and large cities (17%), and professional homes (34%), managerial homes (35%), and blue collar/clerical homes (25%).

When asked about their sexual orientation, 77% replied that they were either predominantly or exclusively homosexual; the rest expressed some heterosexual interest, although also claiming to be gay or lesbian. Many chose to remain closeted, to a few heterosexuals (49%), a large number of heterosexuals (27%), or everyone (4%). Forty-one percent of the youths seldom went to a bar (once a month or less), 58% attended an organized gay activity as frequently, 56% did not subscribe to a gay or lesbian periodical, and 89% were not active participants in the gay rights movement. Slightly less than half were involved in a self-defined love affair at the time of data collection, while the same percentage had had fewer than five homosexual sexual experiences.

Six (6%) of the lesbians and 18 (8%) of the gay males did not complete one of the dependent variables (known to parents or self-esteem) investigated in this study. They were dropped from further analyses.

Measures

Gay and Lesbian Questionnaire (GAL Q). To assess the variables of interest, existing questionnaires were examined for appropriateness with a youthful population. A fairly brief (15 to 30 minutes) instrument was desired in order to increase the return rate. Items from the Blumstein-Schwartz (1983) and Weinberg-Williams (1974) questionnaires were deemed appropriate and were included, as well as several original questions concerning parenting, love affairs, physical development, and athletics, to form a 10-page questionnaire (GAL Q).

Rosenberg Self-Esteem Scale (RSE). The RSE (Rosenberg, 1979) is a commonly used 10-item Likert-type scale that addresses issues of global self-esteem (e.g., "On the whole, I am satisfied with myself"), explicitly distinct from specific contexts. The 4-step scoring method (Schilling & Savin-Williams, in preparation) has a person separation index of .89. Inter-item reliability and the RSE's correlation with other self-report, self-esteem scales are consistently high (Demo, 1985; Savin-Williams & Demo, 1984).

Procedures

In distributing the GAL Qs and the RSEs, my primary concern was to sample youths from a variety of sources. A summer picnic sponsored by the local gay bar, The Common Ground, was the first major event in which the GAL Qs were given to prospective participants. Although there were over 200 in attendance from the Southern Tier region of New York state, most were older than 23 years of age, the predetermined upper age limit for inclusion as youth. Only 7% of the eventual sample of 317 was recruited at the community picnic.

The GAL Qs were also distributed at three college campus meetings: SUNY Binghamton (NY), University of Minnesota, and Iowa State. All in attendance, numbering 49 (15% of the total), completed the GAL Q. At a gay and lesbian activist conference held in Ithaca, New York, and attended by 180 students from New England and Mid-Atlantic states, 62 of the 67 youths in a workshop that I conducted returned a completed GAL Q (20%). Six (2%) students in a Cornell University human sexuality course who rated themselves between 2 and 6 on the Kinsey scale were included in the sample; they were among 200 students in the class.

The major source (43%) of respondents was the friendship networks of the five undergraduate research assistants for the project and myself. We gave the GAL Qs to friends and asked those friends to distribute the questionnaires to their friends. A preaddressed, postage-free envelope was included, providing a convenient and anonymous technique for those who might feel uncomfortable with their responses or with others knowing of their participation. To increase geographic diversity, each of us sent 10 questionnaires to friends in other states requesting that they give the GAL Q to gays and lesbians under 23 years of age. Forty-three (14%) were returned from several states in the Midwest, South, and East.

Variables

Self-esteem. Evaluation of the self was assessed by the Rosenberg Self-Esteem Scale (RSE). From "strongly agree" to "strongly disagree," respondents indicated the degree to which the five positively stated and five negatively stated sentences characterized them.

Parental knowledge of their child's homosexuality. In response to the GAL Q question, "Do the following people know that you are gay?", the youths indicated one of four responses: "definitely knows and we have talked about it," "definitely knows but we have never talked about it," "probably knows or suspects," or "does not know or suspect." Included in the list of people were "your mother" and "your father." This variable is the *youth's knowledge* of whether or not the parent knows.

Satisfaction with maternal and paternal relationship. On a scale from "extremely satisfied" (1) to "not at all satisfied" (9), the youths answered, "How satisfied are you with your relationship with your parents?" The mother and father were assessed separately.

Contact with parents. One of nine categories was selected by the youths in response to the GAL Q question, "Overall, how often do you have any kind of contact (by phone, mail, visits, etc.) with your mother/father?'' The range was from ''daily to almost every day'' (1) to ''once a month'' (5) to ''never'' (9).

Parents' marital status. The youths indicated if their biological parents were currently married, separated, or divorced.

Age of parents. From the GAL Q question, ''How old are your parents?'', the age of the mother and father was assessed.

Data Analysis

Data analysis proceeded in four steps:

1. Descriptive accounts of the dependent and independent variables.
2. Intercorrelations among the study's variables.
3. Regression of the independent variables on parental knowledge of their son's or daughter's homosexuality.
4. Regression of the above variables on the self-esteem of the youths.

In addition, Item 4 above was repeated separately for each age, community, occupational status, and sexual orientation group. Although the number of cases was too small for valid confirmatory data analyses, the regression results serve as suggestive findings for future research. All analyses were conducted separately for sex of youth and of parent. Regression procedures were standard, least-squares linear regressions derived from the SAS program.

RESULTS

Descriptive Data

Table 1 presents the raw data and means for all study variables. There were relatively few differences between gay and lesbian youths. Females were slightly more satisfied with parental relationships, but they had less contact with them than did males; males were more out to their fathers than lesbians were to their fathers. The lesbians, in turn, had a slightly higher self-esteem level than did the male youths.

As might be expected, mothers were younger than fathers, and

TABLE 1. Frequency and Percent of Total for the Independent Variables for Male and Female Youth.

Variable	Frequency		Percent of Total	
	Males	Females	Males	Females
Satisfaction with Father				
1 (High)	13	5	7	5
2	20	12	10	13
3	24	16	12	17
4	15	6	8	6
5	24	9	12	9
6	30	14	15	15
7	29	10	15	10
8	24	16	12	17
9 (Low)	21	8	11	8
Mean	5.37	5.24		
Satisfaction with Mother				
1 (High)	27	13	13	13
2	37	18	18	18
3	41	24	20	24
4	28	14	14	14
5	23	5	11	5
6	23	8	11	8
7	10	8	5	8
8	12	7	6	7
9 (Low)	6	3	3	3
Mean	3.98	3.92		

Contact with Father

1 (Frequent)	22	5	11	5
2	9	5	4	5
3	54	22	26	23
4	66	38	32	39
5	23	11	9	11
6	18	13	9	13
7	4	1	2	1
8	2	1	1	1
9 (Infrequent)	6	1	3	1
Mean	3.84	4.04		

Contact with Mother

1 (Frequent)	28	8	13	8
2	16	7	8	7
3	78	38	37	38
4	59	36	28	36
5	15	8	7	8
6	10	2	5	2
7	1	0	1	0
8	0	1	0	1
9 (Infrequent)	2	0	1	0
Mean	3.32	3.40		

TABLE 1 (continued)

Variable	Frequency		Percent of Total	
	Males	Females	Males	Females
Parents Married				
Yes	166	68	77	66%
No	44	34	21	33%
Father's Age				
30s	8	4	4	4%
40s	75	35	35	34%
50s	91	48	43	47%
60s +	26	10	12	10%
Mean	51.36	51.06		
Mother's Age				
30s	13	6	6	6%
40s	101	50	47	48%
50s	78	36	37	35%
60s +	13	7	6	7%
Mean	48.74	48.57		

Father Knows				
1 (Yes)	80	26	37	25
2	11	16	5	16
3	46	17	21	17
4 (No)	65	38	30	37
Mean	2.41	2.71		
Mother Knows				
1 (Yes)	98	47	46	46
2	16	13	7	13
3	42	20	20	19
4 (No)	53	20	25	19
Mean	2.15	2.14		
Self-Esteem				
range	8-30	10-30		
mean	21.98	22.18		

the youths reported greater satisfaction and more contact with mothers. Fathers were less likely to know of their child's sexual orientation than were mothers.

Correlation of All Variables

Females. Table 2 presents the intercorrelations of all study variables for the lesbians. In general, there was high congruency in the data a lesbian reported for mothers and fathers on the same dimension. Thus, if mother knew, father knew; if the youth was satisfied with her relationship with mother and had frequent contact with her, then she was also satisfied with her paternal relationship and had frequent contact with him. Also, the ages of the parents were highly correlated with each other.

Contact with a parent was highly correlated with satisfaction with that parent. If the parents were married, then they were more likely to be of advanced age and it was more likely for their daughter to have contact and to be satisfied with the mother (but not the father).

Young mothers and fathers were most likely to know that their daughter is a lesbian. In addition, a lesbian who reported that her father knew her sexual orientation was most likely to have a good relationship with him. Only two variables were significantly correlated with a lesbian's self-esteem: a young mother and satisfaction with the maternal relationship. These two were not, however, highly correlated with each other.

Males. The data for the gay male youths are presented in Table 3. Similar to lesbians, all mother-father comparable data (knows, contact, satisfaction, age) were significantly correlated with each other.

Contact with the father was significantly correlated with a youth's report of satisfaction with their relationship; no similar trend was found for the mother. A gay male expressed better relationships with young parents than older ones, and he had more contact with married than with divorced or separated parents.

A male with high self-esteem reported satisfying relationships with both parents and having a mother who knows his sexual orientation. No other variable significantly correlated with parental knowledge of the son's homosexuality.

Regression: Parents' Knowledge of Child's Sexual Orientation

Females. A lesbian's report that her parents know her sexual orientation was significantly predicted by the proposed model for mothers ($F = 2.93$, 4 df, $p = .025$, $r^2 = 11\%$) and fathers ($F = 3.20$, 4 df, $p = .017$, $r^2 = 13\%$). The best mother predictors were a young maternal age ($t = 2.22$, $p = .029$) and the daughter's report of a satisfying relationship with her ($t = 1.63$, $p = .106$). The same variables also predicted fathers' knowledge: young paternal age ($t = 2.44$, $p = .017$) and satisfaction ($t = 1.92$, $p = .056$).

Males. Neither the maternal ($F = .71$, 4 df, $p = .588$, $r^2 = 2\%$) nor the paternal ($F = .99$, 4 df, $p = .415$, $r^2 = 2\%$) model significantly predicted a gay youth's report of parental knowledge of his homosexuality. Only one individual item, satisfaction with paternal relationship ($t = 1.77$, $p = .079$), approached significance.

Regression: The Self-Esteem of Youth

Females. The mother ($F = 3.27$, 5 df, $p = .009$, $r^2 = 15\%$), but not the father ($F = 1.06$, 5 df, $p = .388$, $r^2 = 6\%$) variables predicted the self-esteem level of lesbians. Two individual items were significant contributors, satisfaction with maternal relationship ($t = -2.54$, $p = .013$) and a young mother ($t = -2.50$, $p = .014$). Two others approached significance, parents married in the mother model ($t = 1.81$, $p = .074$) and a young father ($t = -1.79$, $p = .077$).

These patterns did not vary by the age, community, family occupational status, or sexual orientation of the lesbians (see Tables 4 and 5).

Males. Both the mother ($F = 4.44$, 5 df, $p = .0008$, $r^2 = 10\%$) and the father ($F = 3.76$, 5 df, $p = .003$, $r^2 = 9\%$) variables significantly predicted the self-esteem level of a gay youth. The best individual predictors were satisfaction with mother ($t = -3.54$, $p = .0005$) and father ($t = -3.42$, $p = .0008$). If the mother knew her son's sexual orientation, his self-esteem was more likely to be positive ($t = -2.38$, $p = .018$); this relationship was not the case if the father knew ($t = -.26$, $p = .797$). Infrequent

TABLE 2. Correlations Between All Variables for Lesbian Youth.

		RSE2	MOMKNOWS	DADKNOWS	PARMARRY
RSE2	r	1.00			
	p	0.00			
	n	97			
MOMKNOWS	r	0.05	1.00		
	p	0.61	0.00		
	n	95	97		
DADKNOWS	r	-0.05	0.46	1.00	
	p	0.61	0.0001	0.00	
	n	92	93	94	
PARMARRY	r	0.08	0.16	-0.08	1.00
	p	0.43	0.12	0.44	0.00
	n	96	97	94	98
MOMAGE	r	-0.23	0.28	0.20	0.26
	p	0.02	0.01	0.05	0.01
	n	94	96	92	96
DADAGE	r	-0.18	0.23	0.25	0.25
	p	0.08	0.02	0.02	0.02
	n	92	93	94	94
CONMOM	r	-0.12	-0.06	-0.13	0.05
	p	0.27	0.59	0.22	0.63
	n	95	97	93	97
CONDAD	r	-0.07	-0.11	0.14	-0.30
	p	0.52	0.31	0.16	0.003
	n	92	93	94	94
SATSFMOM	r	-0.26	0.19	-0.04	0.16
	p	0.01	0.07	0.73	0.11
	n	95	97	93	97
SATSFDAD	r	-0.16	0.01	0.25	-0.26
	p	0.14	0.96	0.01	0.01
	n	91	92	93	93

MOMAGE	DADAGE	CONMOM	CONDAD	SATSFMOM	SATSFDAD
1.00					
0.00					
96					
0.84	1.00				
0.0001	0.00				
92	94				
0.00	0.12	1.00			
0.98	0.24	0.00			
96	93	97			
−0.07	0.05	0.46	1.00		
0.53	0.65	0.0001	0.00		
92	94	93	94		
0.15	0.16	0.30	−0.11	1.00	
0.13	0.11	0.003	0.31	0.00	
96	93	97	93		
0.08	0.05	0.01	0.34	0.31	1.00
0.45	0.63	0.91	0.0001	0.003	0.00
91	93	92	93	92	93

TABLE 3. Correlations Between All Variables for Gay Male Youth.

		RSE2	MOMKNOWS	DADKNOWS	PARMARRY
RSE2	r	1.00			
	p	0.00			
	n	196			
MOMKNOWS	r	-0.15	1.00		
	p	0.03	0.00		
	n	193	195		
DADKNOWS	r	-0.04	0.72	1.00	
	p	0.63	0.0001	0.00	
	n	190	188	191	
PARMARRY	r	0.05	-0.03	-0.03	1.00
	p	0.52	0.68	0.64	0.00
	n	194	193	190	196
MOMAGE	r	-0.07	0.01	-0.01	0.12
	p	0.35	0.92	0.91	0.09
	n	189	191	184	189
DADAGE	r	-0.08	0.02	0.04	0.14
	p	0.28	0.77	0.60	0.06
	n	188	186	187	189
CONMOM	r	0.08	-0.06	-0.01	-0.26
	p	0.26	0.43	0.94	0.00
	n	193	195	188	193
CONDAD	r	0.10	0.06	0.05	-0.36
	p	0.17	0.41	0.48	0.00
	n	192	190	190	193
SATSFMOM	r	-0.22	0.03	-0.05	0.08
	p	0.003	0.73	0.48	0.26
	n	191	193	186	191
SATSFDAD	r	-0.22	-0.01	0.14	-0.12
	p	0.002	0.85	0.06	0.11
	n	189	187	187	190

MOMAGE	DADAGE	CONMOM	CONDAD	SATSFMOM	SATSFDAD
1.00					
0.00					
191					
0.87	1.00				
0.0001	0.00				
185	189				
0.12	0.09	1.00			
0.09	0.20	0.00			
191	186	195			
0.06	0.02	0.63	1.00		
0.44	0.83	0.0001	0.00		
186	189	190	193		
0.16	0.19	0.13	−0.01	1.00	
0.03	0.01	0.07	0.86	0.00	
190	185	193	188	193	
−0.10	−0.03	0.00	0.15	0.36	1.00
0.20	0.71	0.96	0.04	0.0001	0.00
184	187	187	190	187	190

TABLE 4. Age, Community, Occupational Status, and Sexual Orientation Variations in Maternal Variables Predicting Lesbian Self-Esteem.

Variable	DF	Sum of Squares	F Values	P Values
Age				
14-19	5	69.18	1.28	.313
20	5	96.68	.97	.466
21	5	97.28	.79	.565
22-23	5	192.69	1.58	.235
Community				
Rural	5	75.40	1.75	.278
Small Town	5	179.94	1.97	.127[1]
Medium Town	5	167.06	2.50	.059[2]
Small City	5	59.56	.66	.665
City	5	10.71	.04	.998

Occupational Status

Professional	5	215.07	1.87	.135[3]
Managerial	5	87.37	.99	.441
Blue Collar	5	94.94	1.19	.346

Sexual Orientation

Significant Heterosexuality	5	100.47	1.03	.417
Predominant Homosexuality	5	58.93	.70	.629
Exclusive Homosexuality	5	53.84	3.00	.027[4]

[1]   Satisfaction with Mother: t = -2.77, p = .012

[2]   Satisfaction with Mother: t = -2.27, p = .032

[3]   Mother's Age: t = -2.20, p = .037

[4]   Satisfaction with Mother: t = -2.15, p = .04

TABLE 5. Age, Community, Occupational Status, and Sexual Orientation Variations in Paternal Variables Predicting Lesbian Self-Esteem.

Variable	DF	Sum of Squares	F Values	P Values
Age				
14-19	5	69.02	1.04	.420
20	5	56.74	.48	.782
21	5	63.97	.51	.765
22-23	5	112.11	.76	.594
Community				
Rural	5	69.14	1.40	.361
Small Town	5	118.67	1.24	.331
Medium Town	5	145.74	2.20	.091
Small City	5	66.87	.76	.595
City	5	81.62	.53	.748

Occupational Status

Professional	5	165.05	1.27	.309
Managerial	5	82.91	.99	.444
Blue Collar	5	39.83	.46	.805

Sexual Orientation

Significant Heterosexuality	5	40.52	.37	.863
Predominant Homosexuality	5	122.52	1.62	.204
Exclusive Homosexuality	5	111.55	1.00	.435

1   Father's Age: t = -2.47, p = .022

contact with father also predicted high self-esteem ($t = 2.60, p = .01$).

Among the six age categories, the models best predicted self-esteem at age 19 (see Tables 6 and 7). Infrequent but satisfying contact with mother predicted high self-esteem among 19-year-olds, many of whom were college freshmen. Frequent contact with mother at age 22 and satisfaction with mother at age 23 predicted positive self-evaluation, ages usually associated with post-college or independent living conditions.

Both maternal and paternal models were highly significant among small town gays, and the maternal model was significant among rural males (see Tables 6 and 7). One interesting contrast was that among rural youths a mother who knew predicted high self-esteem, whereas among urban youths, infrequent contact with mother had that effect.

The predictive power of the independent variables was significant or approached significance regardless of the occupational status of the gay males' family (see Tables 6 and 7). Satisfying parental relationships were particularly important in predicting self-esteem level among professional status youths; infrequent contact with parents and married parents, among managerial status youths. In blue collar homes, those with the highest self-esteem levels had mothers who knew of their homosexuality. The family variables predicted self-esteem only among males who reported that they are exclusively gay (see Tables 6 and 7).

DISCUSSION

Lesbians who reported satisfying relationships with their parents and who had relatively young parents were most likely to be out to their parents. This is consistent with the coming out advice literature. Unsuccessful, however, was the attempt to predict characteristics of the parents and of the parental relationships of male youths who reported that they were out to their parents. This difference was apparent despite the fact that the lesbians and gay males did not vary in their responses to the independent variables.

The self-esteem level of the youths was highly predictive from the maternal (both sexes) and the paternal (males only) models. Gay and lesbian youths who reported satisfying relationships with their mothers had the highest levels of self-esteem. In addition, a young mother was conducive to a positive self-image for lesbians, while gay males who were out to their mother and who had a satisfying but infrequent relationship with their father were most likely to report high self-esteem.

As suggested by the subgroup regression analyses, these relationships were strongest for gay males who claimed to be exclusively homosexual and who were raised in small towns, perhaps an artifact of the large number of cases in these two groups. A mother who knows best predicted high self-esteem among gay males from blue collar and rural homes, whereas satisfaction with both parents best predicted high self-esteem among those from professional and small town homes. Although satisfaction with mother appeared to be related to high self-esteem for all ages of gay youths, among the adolescents infrequent mother contact (an indication of freedom?) also predicted high self-esteem, whereas among older youths frequent mother contact (an indication of renewed ties?) best indicated high self-esteem. Little contact with parents was most highly related to positive self-evaluations for gay males from upwardly mobile urban homes. It is important to remember that because of the small number of cases in these analyses, the findings are only suggestive and should be more systematically pursued in future studies.

A potentially interesting question raised by the analyses is to explore why the subdivisions into groups based on age, home town community, occupational family status, and sexual orientation differentiated gay males far more than lesbians. Also, for both males and females and in both mother and father acceptance models, the widest within group variations occurred in the community and sexual orientation groups, indicating the potential usefulness of these divisions in noting the significance of psychological variables. They proved far more useful than age (except for gay males in the maternal model) and family occupational status. In particular, the distinction was greatest between a rural/small town heritage and an urban childhood background, and between exclusively homosexual and significantly heterosexual (especially for males) individuals. Clearly, it is misleading to group all gays and lesbians together, especially when examining psychosocial issues, the primary goal of

TABLE 6. Age, Community, Occupational Status, and Sexual Orientation Variations in Maternal Variables Predicting Gay Male Self-Esteem.

Variable	DF	Sum of Squares	F Values	P Values
Age				
14-18	5	154.07	.94	.473
19	5	336.00	3.19	.023[1,2,3]
20	5	211.44	2.11	.093
21	5	154.72	1.22	.320
22	5	122.63	1.00	.437[4]
23	5	310.49	2.41	.082[5]
Community				
Rural	5	343.99	2.58	.046[6]
Small Town	5	336.43	2.80	.029[7,8]
Medium Town	5	99.70	.91	.484
Small City	5	38.18	.22	.950
City	5	145.13	1.17	.348[9]
Occupational Status				
Professional	5	270.19	1.83	.120[10]
Managerial	5	327.50	2.58	.034[11,12]
Blue Collar	5	376.70	5.59	.001[13,14]

Sexual Orientation

Significant Heterosexuality	5	82.77	.58	.714
Predominant Homosexuality	5	195.71	1.24	.300
Exclusive Homosexuality	5	470.22	4.88	.001 15,16

1 Satisfaction with Mother: t = -2.54, p = .018
2 Contact with Mother: t = 3.17, p = .004
3 Parents Married: t = 2.05, p = .051
4 Contact with Mother: t = -2.17, p = .041
5 Satisfaction with Mother: t = -2.31, p = .034
6 Mother Knows: t = -3.03, p = .005
7 Satisfaction with Mother: t = -2.73, p = .009
8 Parents Married: t = 2.06, p = .046
9 Contact with Mother: t = 2.14, p = .042
10 Satisfaction with Mother: t = -2.65, p = .010
11 Contact with Mother: t = 2.60, p = .012
12 Parents Married: t = 2.29, p = .026
13 Satisfaction with Mother: t = -2.34, p = .025
14 Mother Knows: t = -3.89, p = .000
15 Mother Knows: t = -1.99, p = .050
16 Satisfaction with Mother: t = -4.06, p = .000

TABLE 7. Age, Community, Occupational Status, and Sexual Orientation Variations in Paternal Variables Predicting Gay Male Self-Esteem.

Variable	DF	Sum of Squares	F Values	P Values
Age				
14-18	5	217.70	1.33	.296
19	5	227.29	1.82	.145[1]
20	5	127.27	1.15	.358[2]
21	5	210.38	1.75	.150[3]
22	5	171.44	1.53	.218
23	5	240.34	1.60	.218
Community				
Rural	5	97.88	.53	.750
Small Town	5	468.69	4.52	.002[4,5,6]
Medium Town	5	126.98	1.17	.338
Small City	5	130.73	1.06	.428
City	5	137.10	1.17	.346
Occupational Status				
Professional	5	405.97	2.95	.018[8]
Managerial	5	345.98	2.89	.021[9,10]
Blue Collar	5	219.05	2.29	.065

Sexual Orientation

Significant Heterosexuality	5	131.96	.94	.483
Predominant Homosexuality	5	221.07	1.39	.240[11]
Exclusive Homosexuality	5	379.58	3.90	.003[12,13]

1 Satisfaction with Father: $t = -2.14$, $p = .042$
2 Parents Married: $t = 2.15$, $p = .04$
3 Satisfaction with Father: $t = -2.11$, $p = .042$
4 Satisfaction with Father: $t = -2.60$, $p = .013$
5 Contact with Father: $t = 3.33$, $p = .002$
6 Parents Married: $t = 2.99$, $p = .005$
7 Father's Age: $t = -3.72$, $p = .001$
8 Satisfaction with Father: $t = -3.65$, $p = .001$
9 Contact with Father: $t = 2.61$, $p = .011$
10 Parents Married: $t = 2.44$, $p = .018$
11 Satisfaction with Father: $t = -2.13$, $p = .038$
12 Satisfaction with Father: $t = -2.23$, $p = .028$
13 Contact with Father: $t = 2.94$, $p = .004$
14 Father's Age: $t = -2.49$, $p = .015$

this study. In this regard, gay and lesbian youth reflect the reality of life in America.

Based on data from this study and an earlier report (Savin-Williams, 1989), positive parental relationships were good predictors of which lesbians felt comfortable with their sexual orientation (parental acceptance of their homosexuality) and were likely to be out to their parents (satisfaction with parental relationships). Compared to responses from gay males, however, relatively few of the tested parental variables were significant predictors of lesbian self-esteem. Only satisfaction with maternal relationship and young parents were related to positive self-evaluation. Seemingly unimportant to their self-esteem were parental acceptance, feeling comfortable with sexual orientation, parental knowledge of their homosexuality, contact with parents, a satisfying relationship with father, and the marital status of the parents.

By contrast, although the parental variables were not related to a gay male youth's report of being out to his parents, they served as excellent correlates of his self-esteem level. If the parents are important to a gay male's sense of self-worth, then their acceptance of his homosexuality predicted his comfortableness with being gay, which in turn significantly predicted his level of self-esteem. In addition, if his parental relationships are satisfying, if his mother knows that he is gay, and if he has relatively little contact with his father, then he reported a positive self-evaluation. Unimportant factors were if the father knows, contact with the mother, age of parents, and the marital status of his parents.

This sex difference is somewhat surprising when one considers traditional psychological literature on psychosocial issues during adolescence. Generally, it is believed that females learn about the self in the context of interpersonal, intimate relationships with others, while males develop their self-conception through more autonomous and independence seeking endeavors (Douvan & Adelson, 1966; Gallatin, 1975; Gilligan, 1982). Recent empirical research, however, casts doubt on these assumptions. For example, Demo, Small, and Savin-Williams (1987) and Gecas and Schwalbe (1986) reported that the self-esteem of boys, compared to that of girls, was more strongly related to various aspects of family relations, such as communication and physical and emotional support. Apparently, the importance of the family for the self-evaluation of youths is characteristic not only of the assumed heterosexual samples of Demo et al. and Gecas and Schwalbe, but also of the explicitly gay and lesbian population included in this study.

A lesbian appeared to be affected by her perception of maternal acceptance of her homosexuality regardless of how important she also reported the mother was for her sense of self-worth, and her self-esteem was predicted by her level of satisfaction with her mother but not her father. The significance of the mother was also apparent for a gay male youth's self-esteem: The maternal model was more highly predictive of the acceptance/comfortableness/self-esteem route (Savin-Williams, 1989) than was the paternal model. For a male youth, out to mother but not to father predicted high self-esteem, and infrequent contact with father predicted positive self-esteem. Perhaps the significance of the mother lies in her unique role as "mother" and the seemingly more distant and less satisfying paternal relationship that many gay males and lesbians reported in this study and in other investigations (see review in Bell, Weinberg, & Hammersmith, 1981).

These mother-father differences do not, however, warrant support for the traditional "dominant mother/aloof father" syndrome proposed as a causative factor in the development of homosexuality by psychoanalytic writers, primarily because similar relationships also characterize heterosexual youth. Rather, a more parsimonious explanation is that for many adolescents in our culture, regardless of sexual orientation, relationship with mother is considerably more supportive, warm, and emotional than is relationship with father (Steinberg, 1985). Apparently, this condition is more likely to occur if the mother is young. For lesbians in this study, having a young mother was significantly correlated, and a significant predictor in the regression analyses, with mother knows of her daughter's homosexuality and with their self-esteem level. Gay males reported the highest levels of satisfaction with young mothers. As suggested by the coming out right literature, the significance of the mother's youthfulness may reside in her own child-rearing culture that allowed her to be more open and tolerant, if not accepting, of homosexuality. This question requires further study.

Several limitations of the present investigation are worth noting, especially in regard to the sampled population and the study's results. Although the participants were quite diverse on a number of dimensions, there were relatively few ethnic minorities included in the population. Also, the sample as a whole was highly educated. Despite the efforts of the female research assistants, our attempt to increase the number of lesbians in the study proved frustrating. This shortage may reflect the lower number of women than men in the gay and lesbian population (see Bell et al., 1981, and Kinsey, Pomeroy, Martin, & Gebhard, 1953), or, as the literature also indicates (e.g., de Monteflores & Schultz, 1978), that women "come out" at a later age than do men. Also, not surprisingly, there were relatively few junior or senior high school age youths in the sample, reflecting the invisibility of gay and lesbian adolescents in society and to researchers, health care providers, and the youths themselves (Savin-Williams, in preparation).

The diversity of the current sample is indicated by the inclusion of individuals who have seldom appeared in previous studies of gays and lesbians of any age: adolescents under the age of 18 years, gays and lesbians with 12 or fewer years of education, those from rural and small towns and from working class homes, those who express significant heterosexual interest, and youths not yet out to anyone or to few others. With a larger population of lesbian and gay youth, future studies could begin to untangle the significance of these characteristics, not only for issues addressed in this paper, but for many others as well; for example, little is known concerning the evolution of the identity process for gay and lesbian youth.

It is important to recognize as well that the findings in the present investigation, even the significant ones, accounted for relatively little (9% to 15% at best) of the variance in coming out to parents and the self-esteem of the youths. Apparently, there are critical factors other than relationships with parents that account for the determination of youths' willingness to come out to their parents and their level of self-evaluation. A more complete analysis of the current data is currently being undertaken to explore the multideterminants of these issues (Savin-Williams, in preparation).

Because data collection was cross-sectional and not longitudinal, any conclusions regarding causation and prediction are tenuous at best. The models tested reflect a theoretical bias, that coming out predicts self-esteem level. Perhaps an equally valid assumption is that self-esteem level determines who is likely to come out. It is also not clear if (a) a satisfying parental relationship encourages a lesbian to come out to her parents, or the relationship is satisfying because the lesbian youth has come out to them; and (b) for a gay male, satisfaction with parents causes or is the result of his high self-esteem. The coming out right advice literature is not particularly helpful because it suggests, in the former case, that both are true: Parental relationships are more likely to be fulfilling and positive once gay or lesbian youths are honest with the parents about their innermost secret and, on the other hand, that a prior good relationship with their parents makes it much easier for lesbian or gay youths to talk to them about the secret.

The theoretical and empirical literature on the coming out process should have been helpful in proposing and testing various causal pathways. Instead, because it largely ignores the role of the parents in the coming out process, it sheds relatively little light on these issues. The contribution of the present research is perhaps most significant in providing data that are especially pertinent in documenting the relationships among parental characteristics, the coming out process, and psychological health.

REFERENCES

Bell, A. P., & Weinberg, M. S. (1978). *Homosexualities: A study of diversity among men and women*. New York: Simon & Schuster.

Bell, A. P., Weinberg, M. S., & Hammersmith, S. K. (1981). *Sexual preference: Its development in men and women*. Bloomington, IN: Indiana University Press.

Blumstein, P., & Schwartz, P. (1983). *American couples: Money, work, sex*. New York: William Morrow.

Borhek, M. (1983). *Coming out to parents*. New York: Pilgrim Press.

Cass, V. C. (1979). Homosexual identity formation: A theoretical model. *Journal of Homosexuality, 4*, 219-235.

Cass, V. C. (1984). Homosexual identity formation: Testing a theoretical model. *Journal of Sex Research, 20*, 143-167.

Clark, D. (1977). *Loving someone gay*. New York: Signet.

Coleman, E. (1981-1982). Developmental stages of the coming out process. *Journal of Homosexuality, 7(2/3)*, 31-43.

Dank, B. M. (1971). Coming out in the gay world. *Psychiatry, 34*, 180-197.

Demo, D. H. (1985). The measurement of self-esteem: Refining our methods. *Journal of Personality and Social Psychology, 48*, 1490-1502.

Demo, D. H., Small, S. A., & Savin-Williams, R. C. (1987). Family relations and the self-esteem of adolescents and their parents. *Journal of Marriage and the Family, 49*, 705-715.

de Monteflores, C., & Schultz, S. J. (1978). Coming out: Similarities and differences for lesbians and gay men. *Journal of Social Issues, 34*, 59-72.

Douvan, E., & Adelson, J. (1966). *The adolescent experience.* New York: John C. Wiley & Sons.

Fairchild, B., & Hayward, N. (1979). *Now that you know.* New York: Harcourt & Brace.

Gallatin, J. (1975). *Adolescence and individuality.* New York: Harper & Row.

Gecas, V., & Schwalbe, M. L. (1986). Parental behavior and adolescent self-esteem. *Journal of Marriage and the Family, 48*, 37-46.

Gilligan, C. (1982). *In a different voice.* Cambridge, MA: Harvard University Press.

Heron, A. (Ed.). (1983). *One teenager in ten.* Boston: Alyson.

Kinsey, A. C., Pomeroy, W. B., Martin, C. E., & Gebhard, P. H. (1953). *Sexual behavior in the human female.* Philadelphia: W. B. Saunders.

Lee, J. A. (1977). Going public: A study in the sociology of homosexual liberation. *Journal of Homosexuality, 3*, 49-78.

MacDonald, G. B. (1983). Exploring sexual identity: Gay people and their families. *Sex Education Coalition News, 5*, 1 & 4.

Martin, A. D. (1982). Learning to hide: The socialization of the gay adolescent. *Adolescent Psychiatry, 10*, 52-65.

McDonald, G. J. (1982). Individual differences in the coming out process for gay men: Implications for theoretical models. *Journal of Homosexuality, 8(1)*, 47-60.

Muchmore, W., & Hanson, W. (1982). *Coming out right: A handbook for the gay male.* Boston: Alyson.

Myrick, F. L. (1974). Homosexual types: An empirical investigation. *The Journal of Sex Research, 10*, 226-237.

Plummer, K. (1975). *Sexual stigma: An interactionist account.* Boston: Routledge & Kegan Paul.

Rosenberg, M. (1979). *Conceiving the self.* New York: Basic Books.

Savin-Williams, R. C. Parental influences on the self-esteem of gay and lesbian youths: A reflected appraisals model. *Journal of Homosexuality, 17(1/2)*, 93-109.

Savin-Williams, R. C. (in preparation). *Forgotten and invisible: Gay and lesbian youth.*

Savin-Williams, R. C., & Demo, D. H. (1984). Developmental change and stability in adolescent self-concept. *Developmental Psychology, 20*, 1100-1110.

Schafer, S. (1976). Sexual and social problems of lesbians. *Journal of Sex Research, 12*, 50-69.

Schafer, S. (1977). Sociosexual behavior in male and female homosexuals: A study in sex differences. *Archives of Sexual Behavior, 6*, 355-364.

Schilling, S. G., & Savin-Williams, R. C. (in preparation). The assessment of adolescent self-esteem stability: A new application of the beeper technology and the Rasch measurement model.

Silverstein, C. (1977). *A family matter: A parents' guide to homosexuality.* New York: McGraw-Hill.

Steinberg, L. (1985). *Adolescence.* New York: Knopf.

Troiden, R. R. (1979). Becoming homosexual: A model of gay identity acquisition. *Psychiatry, 42*, 362-373.

Troiden, R. R. (1989). The formation of homosexual identities. *Journal of Homosexuality, 17*(1/2), 43-73.

Weinberg, G. (1972). *Society and the healthy homosexual.* New York: St. Martin's Press.

Weinberg, M. S., & Williams, C. J. (1974). *Male homosexuals: Their problems and adaptations.* New York: Penguin.

Weinberg, T. S. (1978). On "doing" and "being" gay: Sexual behavior and homosexual male self-identity. *Journal of Homosexuality, 4*, 143-156.

"You're a What?":
Family Member Reactions
to the Disclosure of Homosexuality

Erik F. Strommen, PhD

Rutgers University

SUMMARY. The present review summarizes what is known about reactions of family members to disclosure of homosexual identity, both within the family of origin and in families where the disclosing member is a spouse or parent. It is suggested that the traumatic nature of family member reaction consists of two related processes: (a) the application of negative values about homosexuality to the disclosing member, and (b) a perception that homosexual identity negates or violates previous family roles. Future research in this complex and understudied area could reveal much about the nature of both homosexual identity and family relationships.

Homosexuality has been a topic of psychological scrutiny since the emergence of psychology as a discipline in the late 1800s. The traditional orientation of homosexuality research has been etiological in nature, with homosexuality being viewed as either a pathological syndrome or as a set of learned pathological behaviors (Morin, 1977; Turnage & Logan, 1975). The removal of homosexuality from the official list of psychopathologies in 1973 (American Psychiatric Association, 1980; Stoller, 1973) brought on a shift in

---

Dr. Strommen is a lecturer in the Department of Psychology at Rutgers University.

The author would like to thank Karen Briefer and Frederick W. Bozett for their thoughtful comments on an earlier draft of this paper.

Correspondence and reprint requests may be addressed to Erik F. Strommen, Department of Psychology, Tillett Hall, Rutgers University, New Brunswick, NJ 08903.

37

research orientation from a clinical focus to one of describing and defining the exact nature of "being homosexual." Homosexual individuals, rather than the abstract entity "homosexuality," have become the object of study. One of the most striking results of this change in perspective has been the somewhat belated discovery that gay people are members of families, not simply isolated case histories. This article reviews the available literature on gay people and their families in an attempt to summarize what is known about how the family reacts to the presence of a homosexual member and what these reactions may reveal about the nature of family relationships.

THE NATURE OF DISCLOSURE

Having to reveal or explicitly identify one's sexual preference to one's family is a familiar topic in research on homosexual identity. Contemporary Americans view homosexuality not simply as an affectional preference, but as an intrinsic social identity. As Warren (1980) put it, "Logically, homosexuality refers to a type of behavior rather than to a condition. However, homosexuals are viewed generally not just as people who do a certain type of thing, but, rather, as people who are a certain type of being" (p. 124). This "certain type of being" is defined as membership in a stigmatized minority that is the subject of severe negative sanctioning in popular social values (Plummer, 1975; Warren, 1980). This negative sanctioning has complex social, historical, and religious origins, and has led to the formation of a distinct satellite culture composed of self-identified gay people (Boswell, 1980; Humphreys & Miller, 1980; Licata & Peterson, 1981). It has also led to the personal and social phenomena of having to "come out" or explicitly declare one's homosexuality as a part of one's identity, in defiance of social values (Dank, 1972; Ponse, 1980; Saghir & Robins, 1973; Weinberg, 1972).

The acquisition of a gay identity appears to be a complex, lengthy process in which the actual disclosure of one's homosexuality to others is a late event (Cass, 1979, 1984). Disclosure becomes necessary because, unlike skin color or gender, which are overt physical indicators of social group membership, homosexuality is a way of feeling and acting; homosexuals are thus "invisible" both as individuals and as a group (Plummer, 1975; Warren, 1974; Weinberg & Williams, 1974). In addition, there exists a "heterosexual assumption" that presumes membership in the heterosexual majority for all individuals, unless otherwise demonstrated (Ponse, 1980). People with homosexual identities are therefore not only invisible to others, but are also actively misclassified by others as heterosexual. Homosexuals are thus required to negate explicitly this classification by disclosing their identity, in order to prevent others from developing and acting on false expectations of their behavior. Here, the term "disclosure" will be used to refer to this explicit revealing of one's sexual preference to others, particularly family members; the term "coming out" will be used only to refer to a gay person's self-realization of his or her homosexuality.

DISCLOSURE TO THE FAMILY OF ORIGIN

Parents

It is generally held that approximately 5 to 10% of the United States population defines itself as predominantly gay or lesbian (Bell & Weinberg, 1978; Kinsey, Pomeroy, & Martin, 1948; Kinsey, Pomeroy, Martin, & Gephard, 1953). These people are obviously somebody's children, and it is not surprising that the parents of homosexuals are the relatives most often discussed in the psychological literature. This focus on parents has its origins in traditional psychoanalytic theory, which has long held that adult homosexuality has its origins in a disturbance of parent-child interactions in early childhood (Bieber, 1962; Buxbaum, 1959). When nonpatient samples of homosexual persons are studied, however, the results for both gay men and lesbians are consistent: Homosexual adults view their parents and their upbringing as positively (or as negatively) as nonpatient heterosexual adults (Robinson, Skeen, Hobson, & Herrman, 1982; Shavelson, Biaggio, Cross, & Lehman, 1980; Siegelman, 1974a, 1974b, 1981).

Parental reaction to disclosure by a child has been studied primarily from a counseling perspective. This appears to be due to the fact that parental reaction is invariably negative, with the disclosure being perceived as a crisis by the family. Weinberg (1972) and Jones

(1978) reported parental reactions as consisting of two facets. The first is the result of the parents applying their negative conceptions of homosexual identity to their child. This creates for the parent a subjective perception that the child is suddenly a stranger, "a member of another species, someone whose essential wants are unrecognizable and different" (Weinberg, 1972, p. 97). This perception apparently stems partly from the misconceptions the parent has about homosexuals (i.e., my son is a child molester, my daughter is a pervert), and partly from the fact that there is no family role for homosexuals; the child's new identity thus cuts him or her off from the family by causing the parents to apply their negative misconceptions to their child, and by negating the previous role or identity the child had as a family member (Collins & Zimmerman, 1983; DeVine, 1984).

The second facet of parent reaction is a direct product of the first, namely, a powerful feeling of guilt and failure. The parents believe that they have somehow caused their child to become homosexual, and are therefore responsible for their child's new, alien identity. Fairchild and Hayward (1979) provided several excellent autobiographical accounts, written by parents of gays and lesbians, which lend support to the theory that viewing the child as unfamiliar or estranged, combined with a feeling of personal responsibility for making the child this way, plunges parents into an emotional and psychological crisis.

Two studies taking a family systems perspective have attempted to identify specific patterns of reaction to a child's disclosure and have tried to isolate the variables that dictate the nature of parental response to disclosure (Collins & Zimmerman, 1983; DeVine, 1984). DeVine (1984) described the family system, particularly parents, as advancing through a series of states of awareness and acceptance of their child's homosexuality: (a) *subliminal awareness*, where the child's gay identity is suspected due to behavioral and communicational patterns; (b) *impact*, characterized by the actual discovery or disclosure, and described by the crisis atmosphere outlined above; (c) *adjustment*, where the child is initially urged to change orientation or keep the homosexual identity a secret, thus maintaining respectability for the family; (d) *resolution*, where the family mourns the loss of the fantasized heterosexual role for the child and dispels negative myths about homosexuality; and finally, (e) *integration*, where a new role for the child, and new behaviors for dealing with the child's gay identity, are enacted.

DeVine is careful to note that the family may stay fixed at any of these levels indefinitely, rather than necessarily achieving the (most desirable) end stage. The movement through these stages is governed by three aspects of the family as a system: the "cohesion" or closeness of family members, the "regulative structures" or rules that govern family member behavior, and the "family themes," or defining values and behaviors that dictate the family's view of themselves and their interaction with the larger community. Collins and Zimmerman (1983) made a similar point, stating that the major factors affecting reaction to a child's disclosure are the regulative structures and "family themes" of the particular family under consideration.

Certain themes are thought to be especially relevant to family reaction to disclosure. Weinberg (1972) identified two potentially conflicting "parenting themes" toward children that he viewed as influencing parental reaction to disclosure: a "love" or acceptance theme, which motivates the parent to try and accept the child's identity, and a "conventionality" theme, which urges parental rejection of the child in accord with social values. DeVine (1984) mentioned three themes that are likely to act as a source of severe conflict: (a) "maintain respectability at all costs," which implies rejecting or censuring the gay family member as a way to avoid loss of status in the community; (b) "as a family we can solve our own problems," which implies a lack of openness to alternative or unfamiliar values and suggests that the deviant family member is a "problem" that needs to be "fixed"; and (c) "be as our religion teaches us to be," which implies rejection of the family member if homosexuality is negatively sanctioned by the family's religious values (DeVine, 1984, p. 11).

Collins and Zimmerman (1983) also reported that religion plays a large part in determining family reaction. This is certainly not surprising: It is well known that both official religious teaching and the social traditions that stem from them negatively sanction homosexual behavior in both sexes (Boswell, 1980; Hiltner, 1980; McNeill, 1976). There is also indirect evidence to suggest that family values as regards traditional sex roles could play a role in family reaction. Individuals possessing rigid, separate roles for the sexes are less likely to be accepting of any gay person, family member or otherwise (MacDonald, 1974; MacDonald & Games, 1974; Storms, 1978; Weinberger & Millham, 1979).

In recommending therapeutic guidelines, both DeVine (1984) and Collins and Zimmerman (1983) agreed that mourning for the lost family member, or the hoped-for role for the child, is to be encouraged. The goal is that a new role, more congruent with reality, may then be substituted for the old. The inability to adopt a new role, however, may result in the family simply casting out the child as an unacceptable family member. If the family member is an adult, or living independently of the parents, this is primarily an emotional tragedy; if the child is an adolescent, it can be much worse. Dank (1972) suggested that coming out and disclosure may be occurring at younger ages in our society, due in part to an increased emphasis on sexuality in general, the tolerance of homosexual behavior, and the availability of information concerning homosexuality. Whether or not this is true, there is disturbing evidence that the dramatic rise in teenage male prostitution in the United States is at least partially due to the casting out of gay adolescents by their parents (Bales, 1985).

Siblings

While researchers have focused attention on the parents in the families of gay persons, there has been little discussion of the effects of disclosure on siblings. Jones (1978) suggested that sibling reactions are similar to those of parents: The sibling views the disclosing member as a stranger, assigning him or her the stigmatized role of homosexual (with all the negative values and misconceptions that entails), and no longer as a family member. There is, however, no guilt or self-blame reported on the part of siblings. The nature of sibling reaction is definitely a topic for future research, for there is evidence that siblings derive identity status as well as intimacy from one another (Schvaneveldt & Ihinger, 1979). The specific variables contributing to sibling reaction, and how they are similar to and different from those affecting parental reaction, could tell us much about the nature of these family relationships. Both Jones (1978) and DeVine (1984) suggested that family members are disclosed to incrementally, one at a time, with the emotionally closest member being told first, and suggested that siblings are disclosed to in advance of parents. This, too, is a topic for future research. If siblings are the first to be disclosed to, their reactions could play a key role in determining parental reaction, either lessening or increasing its severity. To date, no research has considered sibling-parent interaction in reactions to disclosure.

Grandparents

The family of origin does not consist solely of parents and siblings. Grandparents are significant members of the family whose influence extends not only over their own children, but their grandchildren as well (Matthews & Sprey, 1985; Troll, 1982). Grandparents as family members have only recently been studied empirically, so it is not surprising that current research on disclosure to the family contains no references to grandparent reactions. It has been shown that different family generations differ in their opinions on family issues, but not on political ones (Douglass, Cleveland, & Maddox, 1974). This finding makes it unclear to what degree grandparent reactions to homosexuality (which has both familial and political aspects) are similar to or different from parental reactions within a given family. Given the complete lack of data on grandparents to date, we simply do not know. As the United States population continues to age, however, grandparents will become an increasingly important segment of society and the family. Their reactions to disclosure by grandchildren is a topic that must be addressed if a complete picture of family reactions is to be assembled.

DISCLOSURE TO SPOUSES AND CHILDREN

Husbands and Fathers

A review of the various nonpatient studies of gay men reveals that the percentage of each sample that has been or currently is married is between 14% and 25%, with 20% being a safe estimate. About half of these marriages produce children, meaning that approximately 10% of gay men are fathers as well (Harry, 1983). The reasons that gay men marry are many, and include (a) belief that homosexuality was only incidental to their identity at the time of marriage; (b) lack of awareness of their homosexuality at the time of marriage; (c) family pressure to marry; (d) belief that marriage was the only way to achieve a happy adult life, regardless of sexual orientation; (e) belief that marriage would help them overcome their homosexuality; (f) a desire for children; and of course, (g) honest love for their spouses (Bell & Weinberg, 1978; Bozett, 1980; Dank, 1972; Jones, 1978; Nugent, 1983).

For many of these men, there is no disclosure to their families, even though they may have come out to themselves and other gay persons, and are actively engaged in at least casual, anonymous sexual encounters, if not a long-term affair with another man (Bozett, 1980, 1981; Humphreys, 1970; Saghir & Robins, 1973; Spada, 1979; Voeller & Walters, 1978). The reasons given for deliberate nondisclosure are both emotional and legal. Concern about the reaction of wives and children, as well as fears about job security and social status, are commonly cited.

Some research has suggested that nondisclosing married homosexual men experience their husband or father role (or both) as incompatible with their homosexual identity (Bozett, 1981; Jones, 1978; Ross, 1971). Similar to parents and siblings, who feel alienated from the homosexual family member, these men seem to experience an alienation from themselves. They feel that their family roles cannot be reconciled with their homosexuality, and that they have two distinct, conflicting identities. There is qualitative evidence to suggest that this conflict results from having internalized the negative values of society toward homosexuality. These men see their homosexual identity as bad or undesirable, and their family identities as good, and are unable to picture the two combined. They report feeling that they are less than ideal husbands and fathers precisely because they must split their lives into two distinct parts (Bozett, 1980; Humphreys, 1970; Ross, 1983). These men are often unhappy with their marriages as well, but report that they stay married because of concern for their children (Bozett, 1980, 1981; Ross, 1971; Saghir & Robins, 1973).

Men who do disclose to their families present a different picture.

There is often a period of casual, anonymous sexual encounters prior to disclosure, accompanied by great personal anxiety over being duplicitous with one's family; the desire to relieve this anxiety plays a role in deciding to disclose (Bozett, 1980, 1981, 1982; Humphreys, 1970). Surprisingly, there has been little systematic research exploring the specific reasons why some men eventually choose to disclose to their wives, and some do not. Bozett (1982) suggested that two variables which contribute to disclosure are the husband's own self-awareness concerning his sexuality and the timing of this awareness with events in the ongoing marriage relationship. Men aware of and acting on their homosexuality prior to marriage reported a gradual distancing from their wives during the tenure of the marriage. Disclosure occurred because these men felt the need to be true to their hidden feelings.

In contrast, men who "awakened" to their homosexual feelings in the course of the marriage tended to experience "sharp conflict," a crisis brought on by their guilt over their homosexual feelings and activity. This guilt led to scapegoating of family members and breakdowns in family communication, prompting disclosure as a resolution to the family disruption. Often a change in the family structure, such as the possibility of a new child, or the children having left the home for college, precipitated this type of sharp conflict disclosure. Although several styles of adaptation to disclosure by spouses have been described, such as an asexual friendship within the marriage, or a semi-open relationship, divorce is the most common reported and expected outcome (Bozett, 1981; Coleman, 1985a; Collins & Zimmerman, 1983; Gochros, 1985; Miller, 1979a; Ross, 1972; Saghir & Robins, 1973).

The specific reactions of wives to disclosure constitutes an understudied area. There is indirect and anecdotal evidence that the wives of disclosing gay men initially react in a manner similar to that of parents. They report feeling as if they "don't know" their husbands, and feel that they have failed as wives or somehow caused their husbands to become homosexual. Lingering hostility and bitterness is uncommon, but has been reported (Bozett, 1981; Gochros, 1985; Miller, 1979a; Ross, 1983). A difficulty with this research, however, is that little detailed work has been done directly with these women; published studies rely predominantly on the disclosing husband as a source of information about the marriage and the spouse's reaction. Yet there have been notable exceptions.

Hatterer (1974), taking a psychoanalytic viewpoint, suggested that the long-term maintenance of a heterosexual woman/homosexual man marriage relies in part upon the woman's need to maintain specific types of relationships with men. She suggested that these women "know but don't know" that the husband is gay (and therefore unable to give them a full, adult heterosexual relationship), and that these women may even gravitate to gay men in order to create and sustain the maladaptive relationship they need. Similarly, Coleman (1985a) noted that many of the wives of the gay men in his sample could be characterized as dependent on the husband, clinging to the marriage even in the face of its obvious inability to provide the type of relationship they desire.

Gochros (1985), reporting on a large sample of wives, found that disclosures were often gradual rather than abrupt, and that women's reactions depended largely on the quality of the relationship between the woman and her husband, the timing of the "official" disclosure in relation to other life stresses (such as childbirth, illness, and so on), and the woman's attitudes toward homosexuality. Once again, the wives' reactions seem reminiscent of those of parents: They report feeling shocked and stunned, and then experience a feeling of self-blame or guilt (Did I do this to myself? Have I failed as a wife?). Gochros suggested that a significant aspect of the wife's reaction is the degree to which her coping mechanisms allow her to sort out the confusion, stress, and new information that accompanies the disclosure. Similar to other studies, she found that more than two-thirds of the marriages in her sample ended in divorce.

Disclosure to children represents another scantily studied topic. Bozett (1980) reported that gay fathers disclose in both direct and indirect ways. Direct disclosure is accomplished through explicit verbal admission. Indirect disclosure involves demonstrating affection for another man in the children's presence, leaving gay-oriented reading material out for children to see, or using other nonexplicit clues. Maddox (1982) and Bozett (1980) both reported that although gay fathers stated that direct disclosure was preferred, it was often motivated by external pressures, such as the need to explain parent divorce or cohabitation with a same-sex partner. This suggests that direct disclosure may be motivated as much by necessity as by a specific desire to be open and honest with the child.

Jones (1978), however, suggested that gay fathers do choose to disclose, but prefer to wait until the child is old enough to comprehend the situation, usually in adolescence. Miller (1979b), although giving no hard numbers on how many of the 40 men in his sample had disclosed to their families, reported that they felt the disclosure had brought them closer to their families by removing an unspoken obstacle in their sharing of personal feelings. This perception was shared by the majority of children interviewed as well. Bozett (1980) reported similar findings from a sample of 18 gay fathers. Gay fathers felt that disclosure was important to their role as fathers, and that nondisclosure created a psychological distance between them and their children. Nondisclosing fathers apparently see this distance as a reasonable price to pay for avoiding the conflict and potential negative sanctioning that would accompany disclosure, especially if their wives were undisclosed to and might be told by the children (Bozett, 1981; Miller, 1979).

Wives and Mothers

Lesbians in heterosexual marriages present a more complex and under-researched picture than gay men. There appear to be fewer lesbians than gay men at all ages (Bell & Weinberg, 1978; Kinsey et al., 1948; Kinsey et al., 1953). However, almost one-third of all lesbians have been married, with approximately half of these marriages producing children (Bell & Weinberg, 1978; Saghir & Robins, 1973; Schafer, 1977). Thus, approximately 16% of lesbians are mothers. Lesbians appear to be more likely to marry, possibly as a consequence of the fact that they come out several years later, on average, than do gay men (Bell & Weinberg, 1978; Saghir & Robins, 1973; Schafer, 1977). Because they realize their homosexuality after the popular marrying ages of 21 to 23, they are more "at risk" for marriage than gay men, who typically come out in their late teens (Harry, 1983; Jones, 1978).

Similar to gay men, lesbians marry for reasons of social conformity, family pressures, desire for a stable family life, and love for their spouses (Hanscombe & Forster, 1982; Kirkpatrick, Smith, & Roy, 1981; Saghir & Robins, 1980). Unlike gay fathers, however, there has been little direct research on how lesbians think about their potentially conflicting identities of wife/mother and homosexual. One gets the impression that lesbians view the mother role as an aspect of their identity as a woman, and therefore do not experience the role conflict that gay men do, but there is no explicit statement to this effect (see, e.g., Hanscombe & Forster, 1982).

How or why lesbians disclose (or don't disclose) to their spouses has not been studied in any detail. Similar to gay men, however, what literature does exist is based completely on the lesbian mother's description of the husband's reaction, rather than on the husband's self-reports. There is indirect evidence that husbands are often not disclosed to, and that when they are, they react in a severe and angry manner. Jones (1978) reported on a husband who was almost physically abusive to his wife in his reaction. Coleman (1985b) suggested that a wife's homosexual feelings are viewed as a kind of infidelity by the husband. Given the typical double standard that a woman's infidelity is worse than a man's, this may be one source of the husband's negative reaction.

Hanscombe and Forster (1982) and Hoeffer (1981) both reported that lesbian mothers fear custody battles with their ex-husbands, suggesting that they have not disclosed, or that if they have, enough animosity exists to result in custody litigation. Similarly, Whittlin (1983) reported that most custody cases which involve homosexual parents (usually lesbian mothers) are initiated because a custodial or visiting parent's homosexuality has been discovered by the ex-spouse. This suggests that the ex-husband's reaction is severe enough for him to seek a legal censuring of his ex-wife. Hanscombe and Forster (1982) reported that the ex-husbands of their lesbian mother sample refused to be interviewed, again suggesting continued animosity toward the lesbian mother.

As far as disclosing to children, Hanscombe and Forster (1982) and Hoeffer (1981) both reported that most lesbian mothers are open with their children about their homosexuality, but do not describe how disclosure was made or what initial effect disclosure had. Similar to the studies of children of gay fathers, however, they did report that the children of lesbians felt disclosure brought them closer to their mothers emotionally. Rand, Graham, and Rawlings (1982), in their study of mental health in single lesbian mothers, did not discuss the family's reactions to disclosure, but did report that disclosure to ex-husband, children, and employer is significantly positively correlated with the psychological well-being of the lesbian mother. This finding is congruent with the gay father literature described above, which reported that disclosing gay fathers were happier than nondisclosing fathers.

Custody Issues

It is worthwhile to consider the scant but significant literature that has appeared on the social and legal ramifications of disclosure to one's family in the context of divorce. Parents and siblings of gay people have no direct legal stake in hiding their family member's homosexuality; the negative effects they face as relatives of a gay person are almost entirely social in nature. The disclosing gay family member, however, faces a number of both social and legal sanctions in current society, ranging from a risk of violent assault to the denial of employment and housing (Marotta, 1981; Miller & Humphreys, 1980). The gay or lesbian parent who discloses to a spouse faces not only these problems, but also unexpected legal difficulties in the courts over the issue of child custody (Pagelow, 1980).

It has been consistently reported that if a parent's homosexuality is raised as a custody issue, it not only becomes the central issue in the custody case, but it makes a ruling in favor of the gay parent significantly less likely (Hitchens, 1980; Maddox, 1982; Whittlin, 1983). Hitchens (1980) identified three major concerns voiced directly and indirectly by judges: (a) that homosexual parents may produce homosexual children, particularly through seduction or molestation; (b) that gay parents may produce gender-deviant children such as transsexuals; and (c) that children living with gay parents will suffer unusually harsh harassment by peers because they live with homosexuals. There is no evidence that the first and second concerns are justified (Golombok, Spencer, & Rutter, 1983; Green, 1978; Green, Mandel, Hotvedt, Gray, & Smith, 1986; Groth & Birnbaum, 1978; Hall, 1978; Hoeffer, 1981; Hotvedt & Mandel, 1982; Kirkpatrick, Smith, & Roy, 1981; Miller, 1979b;

Miller, Jacobsen, & Bigner, 1981; Pagelow, 1980; Weeks, Derdeyn, & Longman, 1975). Isolated cases of the third concern, harassment by peers, have been reported (a single child in Bozett, 1980, the son of a gay man; 3 out of 37 children of both lesbians and gay men surveyed in Green, 1978); however, no differences in popularity or friendship patterns have been found for these children, at least for those living with lesbian mothers (Hotvedt & Mandel, 1982; Golombok et al., 1983). Apparently, both gay men and lesbians advise their children to be discreet in disclosing about their parents to others, and they themselves report discretion in their behavior around their children's friends (Golombok et al., 1983; Jones, 1978; Miller, 1979b).

The above studies provide evidence that the courts appear to have legally formalized the same conflict between family roles and a stigmatized homosexual identity that is present as a psychological event in the family. The courts act under many of the same false assumptions and misconceptions about homosexuality that family members do, and often deny custody to homosexual parents based on these assumptions. The courts thus perceive a homosexual identity as incompatible with family roles, particularly the parenting role. The creation of parental homosexuality as a custody issue suggests that the psychological reality of the homosexual identity/family role conflict is powerful enough to convert it into a social and legal reality as well.

CONCLUSIONS

Although our knowledge of how families respond to the disclosure of homosexual identity by a family member is at best fragmentary and incomplete, it is possible to suggest a broad model encompassing all family member reactions. In its most general form, this model has three specific components: (a) the values concerning homosexuality currently held by the family members disclosed to, (b) the effect these values are perceived to have on the relationship between the disclosing family member and other family members, and (c) the conflict resolution mechanisms available to the family members.

Clearly, the most significant aspect of the present model is the values the family members hold concerning homosexuality. It is the implications of these values that form the basis for family member reaction. Given the popular negative sanctioning of homosexual behavior and identity, it is not surprising that family members react strongly when one of their own reveals a homosexual identity. The particular negative values held by individual family members can be expected to show some consistency, depending on which family members are being disclosed to. The members of the family of origin, parents, siblings, and most likely grandparents, can be thought to share the same values: They are united by the themes or values that the family itself identifies with. Due to these shared values, reactions could be very similar within the family. The values held by spouses cannot be predicted, except to the degree that, in conformity with social values, they will tend to be negative to some degree. The values held by the children of homosexual persons represents a very ambiguous topic. Young children cannot be expected to have any distinct values concerning homosexuality; school-age children and adolescents are another matter. This is definitely a topic for future research. To the degree that children internalize popular social values as they mature, we may expect that as their values become more "adult," the potential for conflict with a disclosing parent will increase.

The values held by family members, and their sources both familial and social, are significant for a model of family member reaction because it is the nature of these values that will determine how family members respond to identifying their relative as "a homosexual." This process of applying the social identity of homosexual to the disclosing member appears to involve imbuing that person with all the (negative) traits one believes apply to homosexuals in general. For the family, the most significant aspect of negative social values concerning homosexuality is the perception that homosexuals are not family members at all. This "familylessness," when applied to a relative, appears to produce a subjective feeling of alienation from the disclosing member on the part of other family members aware of the homosexual identity. For parents, this alienation is accompanied by feelings of guilt and personal responsibility for the alienation itself. This reaction strikes the present author as only natural. Parents believe they contribute to their child's personality and achievements in most circumstances, and therefore it is not surprising that they react with feelings of failure when their child discloses a stigmatized identity that the parents themselves do not understand (and may even fear), and for which the family has no role.

The perceived incompatibility of a homosexual identity and a family role is also apparent in spousal reactions to disclosure. Although a much less studied topic, there is evidence that spouses experience the same alienation as parents, based on their own misconceptions about homosexuality, which they apply to the disclosing spouse. Similar to parents, they may also feel responsible or as if they have failed, but failed as spouses, not as parents. It should be noted that this description appears to hold for the wives of gay men; the husbands of lesbians have not been studied in sufficient detail for it to be known if they react in a similar manner. Given the apparent animosity that ex-husbands appear to have for their lesbian ex-wives, it is possible to hypothesize that they react very negatively to their perceived failure as husbands, but this is only speculation. Detailed information on these men's reactions is definitely needed.

Although the children of gays and lesbians have been the subject of much legal and psychological research aimed at assessing their mental health, little is known thus far about how these children conceive of homosexual identity, what their reactions to parental disclosure are, or how their parent's homosexuality affects them. The qualitative appraisals of researchers, as well as self-reports by the children and their parents that are available, imply that disclosure improved the parent-child relationship with the disclosing adult. This is a result in striking contrast to that found for adult disclosure to adult relatives. Are children's values and role expectations more diffuse, and as such more open to adult homosexuality than those of adults? Or have they not yet developed a strong negative conception of homosexuals that would alienate them from their parents? The reported fact that children appreciate the need for discretion suggests that they understand that others view homosexuality negatively. How these children view family roles in relation to sexual preference is definitely a topic for future work.

Perhaps the least studied and least understood feature of the present model is the role of conflict-resolution mechanisms. Whether it involves the family of origin or the marital family, disclosure is always a stressful, if not disruptive, event for family members. Because the social stereotypes for homosexuals do not include family relationships (but do include a plethora of undesirable traits), heterosexual family members find themselves alienated from the disclosing member's new identity. In short, the family members experience a conflict between their identity and role expectations for the disclosing member and the actual homosexual identity the member has adopted. The available research on the family of origin suggests the importance of regulative structures for the resolution of this conflict, and also implies that family themes dictate conflict-resolution strategies in addition to defining family member attitudes toward homosexuality. Empirical reports on the long-term outcomes of disclosure conflicts in the family of origin are lacking, however, so how specific themes are related to particular resolution strategies is not known. The literature on disclosure to spouses and children suggests a greater flexibility in resolution strategies, indicated by the broad variety of compromise living arrangements reported by these families. How these arrangements are chosen is a definite topic for future research, for it would shed much light on conflict resolution within marital families.

Finally, it is worth pausing to consider the concept of disclosure as currently formulated. The studies reviewed above all appear to regard disclosure as the deliberate revealing of one's sexual preference to others, which is assumed to be a voluntary act. This definition suggests that disclosure of sexual identity should be thought of as a particular example of the general phenomena of self-disclosure, which is the volunteering of highly personal information in the context of interpersonal relationships. Many studies in a variety of areas have suggested that self-disclosure enhances personal integrity, social interactions, and intimacy (Chelune et al., 1979; Derlega & Chaikin, 1975; Jourard, 1971). Corroborating evidence that self-disclosure is beneficial to psychological health can be seen in the finding that disclosure of sexual identity, at least for homosexual parents, is beneficial to their psychological well-being. Several studies report gay and lesbian parents as feeling that they "should" disclose. How and why these persons decide to disclose, or perhaps more significantly, decide not to disclose, given the potentially positive effects of self-disclosure for the individual who discloses, is a topic that must be studied in more detail. Presumably, the decision not to disclose relies in part on perceived family reaction, but this is not at all clear.

The decision not to disclose, or perhaps the avoidance of disclosure, raises a largely unstudied possibility: discovery rather than disclosure. Most studies do not distinguish between accidental discovery and voluntary disclosure. Is family reaction different if a family member's homosexuality is inadvertently discovered, rather than deliberately disclosed? What effect does this have on the discovered member, in contrast to the disclosing one? These questions show how much is yet to be learned about how homosexual persons deal with their families, not only in disclosure situations, but on a day-to-day basis.

A homosexual identity presents a unique situation for the family. Homosexuals are not generally viewed as having families, and are the subject of severe negative social sanctioning. When an intimate family member discloses a homosexual identity, the result is a family whose members see the disclosing member's previous role as negated. The individual family members then strive to redefine their relationship with the homosexual member, who they now treat as an embodiment of their own misconceptions about homosexuality. By studying these families, not from a clinical but from a theoretical perspective, it is possible to gain a better understanding not only of general stereotypes of homosexuality, but also of what homosexuality means to particular family roles.

REFERENCES

American Psychiatric Association. (1980). *Diagnostic and statistical manual of mental disorders* (3rd ed.). Washington, DC: Author.

Bales, J. (1985). Gay adolescents' pain compounded. *APA Monitor, 16*(12), 21.

Bell, A. P., & Weinberg, M. S. (1978). *Homosexualities: A study of diversity among men and women.* New York: Simon & Schuster.

Bieber, I. (1962). *Homosexuality.* New York: Basic Books.

Boswell, J. (1980). *Christianity, social tolerance, and homosexuality.* Chicago: University of Chicago Press.

Bozett, F. W. (1980). Gay fathers: How and why they disclose their homosexuality to their children. *Family Relations, 29*, 173-179.

Bozett, F. W. (1981). Gay fathers: Evolution of the gay-father identity. *American Journal of Orthopsychiatry, 51*, 552-559.

Bozett, F. W. (1982). Heterogeneous couples in heterosexual marriages: Gay men and straight women. *Journal of Marital and Sexual Therapy, 8*, 81-89.

Buxbaum, E. (1959). Psychosexual development: The oral, anal, and phallic phases. In M. Levitt (Ed.), *Readings in psychoanalytic psychology* (pp. 43-55). New York: Appleton.

Cass, V. (1979). Homosexual identity formation: A theoretical model. *Journal of Homosexuality, 4*, 219-236.

Cass, V. (1984). Homosexual identity formation: Testing a theoretical model. *Journal of Sex Research, 20*, 143-167.

Chelune, G. J., Archer, R. C., Civikly, J. M., Derlega, V. J., Doster, J. A., Grzelak, J., Herron, J. R., Kleinke, C. L., Nesbitt, J. G., Rosenfeld, L. B., Taylor, D. A., & Waterman, J. (1979). *Self-disclosure: Origins, patterns, and implications of openness in interpersonal relationships.* San Francisco: Jossey-Bass.

Coleman, E. (1985a). Integration of male bisexuality and marriage. *Journal of Homosexuality, 11*(1/2), 189-207.

Coleman, E. (1985b). Bisexual women in marriages. *Journal of Homosexuality, 11*(1/2), 87-99.

Collins, L., & Zimmerman, N. (1983). Homosexual and bisexual issues. In J. C. Hansen, J. D. Woody, & R. H. Woody (Eds.), *Sexual issues in family therapy* (pp. 82-100). Rockville, MD: Aspen Publications.

Dank, B. M. (1972). Why homosexuals marry women. *Medical Aspects of Human Sexuality, 6*, 14-23.

Dank, B. M. (1979). Coming out in the gay world. In M. P. Levine (Ed.), *Gay men* (pp. 103-133). New York: Harper & Row.

Derlega, V., & Chaikin, A. (1975). *Sharing intimacy: What we reveal to others and why.* Englewood Cliffs, NJ: Prentice-Hall.

DeVine, J. L. (1984). A systemic inspection of affectional preference orientation and the family of origin. *Journal of Social Work & Human Sexuality, 2*, 9-17.

Douglass, E., Cleveland, W., & Maddox, G. (1974). Political attitudes, age and aging: A cohort analysis of archival data. *Journal of Gerontology, 29*, 660-675.

Fairchild, B., & Hayward, N. (1979). *Now that you know: What every parent should know about homosexuality.* New York: Harvester/Harcourt Brace Jovanovich.

Gochros, J. S. (1985). Wives' reactions to learning that their husbands are bisexual. *Journal of Homosexuality, 11*(1/2), 101-113.

Golombok, S., Spencer, A., & Rutter, M. (1983). Children in lesbian and single-parent households: Psychosexual and psychiatric appraisal. *Journal of Child Psychology, Psychiatry, and Allied Disciplines, 24*, 551-572.

Green, R. (1978). Sexual identity of 37 children raised by homosexual or trans-sexual parents. *American Journal of Psychiatry, 135*, 692-697.

Green, R., Mandel, J. B., Hotvedt, M. E., Gray, J., & Smith, L. (1986). Lesbian mothers and their children: A comparison with solo heterosexual mothers and their children. *Archives of Sexual Behavior, 15*, 167-184.

Groth, A. N., & Birnbaum, H. J. (1978). Adult sexual orientation and attraction to underage persons. *Archives of Sexual Behavior, 7*, 175-181.

Hall, M. (1978). Lesbian families: Cultural and clinical issues. *Social Work, 23*, 380-385.

Hanscombe, G., & Forster, J. (1982). *Rocking the cradle*. Boston: Alyson.

Harry, J. (1983). Gay male and lesbian relationships. In E. Macklin & R. Rubin (Eds.), *Contemporary families and alternative lifestyles* (pp. 216-234). Beverly Hills, CA: Sage Publications.

Hatterer, M. S. (1974). The problems of women married to homosexual men. *American Journal of Psychiatry, 131*, 275-278.

Hiltner, S. (1980). Homosexuality and the churches. In J. Marmor (Ed.), *Homosexual behavior* (pp. 219-231). New York: Basic Books.

Hitchens, D. (1980). Social attitudes, legal standards, and personal trauma in child custody cases. *Journal of Homosexuality, 5*, 89-95.

Hoeffer, B. (1981). Children's acquisition of sex-role behavior in lesbian-mother families. *American Journal of Orthopsychiatry, 51*, 552-559.

Hotvedt, M. E., & Mandel, J. (1982). Children of lesbian mothers. In J. Weinrich, B. Paul, J. C. Gonsiorek, & M. E. Hotvedt (Eds.), *Homosexuality: Social, psychological, and biological issues* (pp. 275-285). Beverly Hills, CA: Sage Publications.

Humphreys, L. (1970). *Tearoom trade*. Chicago: Aldine.

Humphreys, L., & Miller, B. (1980). Identities in the emerging gay culture. In J. Marmor (Ed.), *Homosexual behavior* (pp. 142-156). New York: Basic Books.

Jones, C. (1978). *Understanding gay relatives and friends*. New York: Seabury Press.

Jourard, S. (1971). *Self-disclosure: An experimental analysis*. New York: John C. Wiley & Sons.

Kirkpatrick, M., Smith, K., & Roy, R. (1981). Lesbian mothers and their children. *American Journal of Orthopsychiatry, 51*, 545-551.

Kinsey, A. C., Pomeroy, W. B., & Martin, C. E. (1948). *Sexual behavior in the human male*. Philadelphia: W. B. Saunders.

Kinsey, A. C., Pomeroy, W. B., Martin, C. E., & Gebhard, P. H. (1953). *Sexual behavior in the human female*. Philadelphia: W. B. Saunders.

Licata, S., & Peterson, R. (Eds.). (1981). *Historical perspectives on homosexuality*. New York: Hawthorne Press.

MacDonald, A. (1974). The importance of sex-role to gay liberation. *Homosexual Counseling Journal, 1*, 169-180.

MacDonald, A., & Games, R. (1974). Some characteristics of those who hold positive and negative attitudes toward homosexuals. *Journal of Homosexuality, 1*, 9-27.

Maddox, B. (1982, February). Homosexual parents. *Psychology Today*, pp. 62-69.

Marotta, T. (1981). *The politics of homosexuality*. Boston: Houghton-Mifflin.

Matthews, S. H., & Sprey, J. (1985). Adolescents' relationship with grandparents: An empirical contribution to conceptual clarification. *Journal of Gerontology, 40*, 621-626.

McNeill, J. (1976). *The church and the homosexual*. Kansas City, MO: Sheed, Andrews, & McMeel.

Miller, B. (1979a). Unpromised paternity: The life-styles of gay fathers. In M. Levine (Ed.), *Gay men* (pp. 239-252). New York: Harper & Row.

Miller, B. (1979b). Gay fathers and their children. *The Family Coordinator, 28*, 544-552.

Miller, B. (1980). Adult sexual resocialization. *Alternative Lifestyles, 1*, 207-232.

Miller, B., & Humphreys, L. (1980). Marginality and violence: Sexual lifestyle as a variable in victimization. *Qualitative Sociology, 3*, 169-185.

Miller, J., Jacobsen, R., & Bigner, J. (1981). The child's home environment for lesbian vs. heterosexual mothers: A neglected area of research. *Journal of Homosexuality, 7*(1), 49-56.

Morin, S. F. (1977). Heterosexual bias in psychological research on lesbianism and male homosexuality. *American Psychologist, 32*, 629-637.

Nugent, R. (1983). Married homosexuals. *Journal of Pastoral Care, 37*, 243-251.

Pagelow, M. (1980). Heterosexual and lesbian single mothers: A comparison of problems, coping, and solutions. *Journal of Homosexuality, 5*, 189-204.

Plummer, K. (1975). *Sexual stigma*. London: Routledge & Kegan Paul.

Ponse, B. (1980). Lesbians and their worlds. In J. Marmor (Ed.), *Homosexual behavior* (pp. 157-175). New York: Basic Books.

Rand, C., Graham, D., & Rawlings, E. (1982). Psychological health and factors the court seeks to control in lesbian mother trials. *Journal of Homosexuality, 8*(1), 27-40.

Robinson, B., Skeen, P., Hobson, C., & Herrman, M. (1982). Gay men's and women's perceptions of early family life and their relationships with their parents. *Family Relations, 31*, 79-83.

Ross, H. (1972). Odd couples: Homosexuals in heterosexual marriages. *Sexual Behavior, 2*, 42-50.

Ross, L. (1971). Mode of adjustment of married homosexuals. *Social Problems, 18*, 385-393.

Ross, M. (1983). *The married homosexual man*. Boston: Routledge & Kegan Paul.

Saghir, M., & Robins, F. (1973). *Male and female homosexuality*. Baltimore: Williams & Wilkins.

Saghir, M., & Robins, F. (1980). Clinical aspects of female homosexuality. In J. Marmor (Ed.), *Homosexual behavior* (pp. 280-295). New York: Basic Books.

Schafer, S. (1977). Sociosexual behavior in male and female homosexuals. *Archives of Sexual Behavior, 6,* 355-364.

Schvaneveldt, J., & Ihinger, M. (1979). Sibling relationships in the family. In W. Burr, R. Hill, F. Nye, & I. Reiss (Eds.), *Contemporary theories about the family. Volume I: Research-based theories* (pp. 453-467). New York: Free Press.

Shavelson, E., Biaggio, M., Cross, H., & Lehman, R. (1980). Lesbian women's perception of their parent-child relationships. *Journal of Homosexuality, 5,* 205-215.

Siegelman, M. (1974a). Parental background of homosexual and heterosexual women. *British Journal of Psychiatry, 124,* 14-21.

Siegelman, M. (1974b). Parental background of male homosexuals and heterosexuals. *Archives of Sexual Behavior, 3,* 3-18.

Siegelman, M. (1981). Parental background of homosexual and heterosexual men: A cross-national replication. *Archives of Sexual Behavior, 10,* 505-513.

Spada, J. (1979). *The Spada report.* New York: Signet Books.

Stroller, R. (1973). A symposium: Should homosexuality be in the APA nomenclature? *American Journal of Psychiatry, 130,* 1207-1216.

Storms, M. (1978). Attitudes toward homosexuality and femininity in men. *Journal of Homosexuality, 3,* 257-266.

Troll, L. (1982). *Continuations: Adult development and aging.* Monterey, CA: Brooks/Cole.

Turnage, J., & Logan, D. (1975). Sexual 'variation' without 'deviation'. *Homosexual Counseling Journal, 2,* 117-120.

Voeller, B., & Walters, J. (1978). Gay fathers. *The Family Coordinator, 27,* 149-157.

Warren, C. (1974). *Identity and community in the gay world.* New York: John C. Wiley & Sons.

Warren, C. (1980). Homosexuality and stigma. In J. Marmor (Ed.), *Homosexual behavior* (pp. 123-141). New York: Basic Books.

Weeks, R., Derdeyn, A., & Longman, M. (1975). Two cases of children of homosexuals. *Child Psychiatry and Human Development, 6,* 26-32.

Weinberg, G. (1972). *Society and the healthy homosexual.* New York: St. Martin's Press.

Weinberg, M. S., & Williams, C. J. (1974). *Male homosexuals: Their problems and adaptations.* New York: Oxford University Press.

Weinberger, L., & Millham, J. (1979). Attitudinal homophobia and support of traditional sex roles. *Journal of Homosexuality, 4,* 237-246.

Whittlin, W. (1983). Homosexuality and child custody: A psychiatric viewpoint. *Conciliation Courts Reviews, 21*(1), 77-79.

Response of Parents to Learning That Their Child Is Homosexual and Concern Over AIDS: A National Study

Bryan E. Robinson, PhD

University of North Carolina at Charlotte

Lynda Henley Walters, PhD
Patsy Skeen, EdD

University of Georgia

SUMMARY. This study was a survey of 402 parents of gay and lesbian children from the northeastern, southern, midwestern, and western regions of the United States. Of particular interest was parental response to the knowledge of their child's homosexuality and the AIDS outbreak. Although parents suffered emotional upset upon learning of their children's homosexuality, many progressed through a five-stage grief process that ended with acceptance. Fear of the spread of AIDS, that their offspring might contract AIDS, or that their child might suffer from the backlash related to AIDS were concerns for most parents. Attitudes toward AIDS were not very different between mothers and fathers. However, older parents were more likely to have more positive attitudes toward AIDS than youn-

Dr. Robinson is Professor of Child and Family Development at the University of North Carolina at Charlotte. Drs. Walters and Skeen are Associate Professors of Child and Family Development at the University of Georgia.

This study was supported in part by funds from the Foundation of the University of North Carolina, the State of North Carolina, and from the Department of Child and Family Development at the University of Georgia.

Correspondence and reprint requests may be addressed to Bryan E. Robinson, Department of Human Services, University of North Carolina at Charlotte, Charlotte, NC 28223.

ger parents, and liberal parents were more likely to have a more positive outlook than their conservative counterparts.

It is estimated that homosexuals and their parents constitute about a third of the population (Woodman, 1985). The relationship between homosexuals and their parents, as well as how parents deal with the fact that their child is homosexual, are therefore important issues for researchers and those in the helping professions to understand. Comments such as "it would just kill my parents," or "I know that I'll lose my parents forever if I come out to them" are frequently made by adult homosexuals (Woodman, 1985, p. 21). It is logical to assume that parents find it difficult to accept their child's homosexuality for several reasons.

Before parents know that their child is homosexual, they assume that the child is part of the accepted heterosexual majority, and plan and dream accordingly. When they learn of the child's homosexuality, they must adjust to the fact that their child is not a part of the majority, but is a part of a minority. Their dreams that their child will have a satisfying traditional marriage, including children, must die. Instead, they must learn to accept a different kind of identity and behavior for their child. It may be that parents experience grief similar to the grief felt by parents whose child has died; they are accepting the "death" of dreams for a heterosexual child and the birth of new dreams and a changed relationship with their homosexual child.

Parents also must come to grips with the fact that the minority to which their child belongs has a long history of persecution. Homosexuality has been condemned in most societies and homosexuals are often persecuted. Although homosexuality is now considered healthy and normal by many, there are still many individuals who consider it a "sick" lifestyle. Homosexuals are victimized also by major religions, the legal system, employers, and members of the helping professions. Such victimization has been attenuated since the discovery of AIDS, initially labeled the "gay plague." Although AIDS is moving rapidly into the heterosexual community, the negative association with homosexuality remains for many, and indeed for parents of homosexuals who must deal with the threat of AIDS, including the possible death of their child.

Research may have also played a part in making the lives of parents of homosexuals difficult. Examinations of relationships of parents with their gay and lesbian children have, in the main, consisted of retrospective accounts of homosexuals who had reached adulthood. These studies have yielded inconsistent findings. Some have supported Freudian theory, indicating that homosexuality is the result of an unhappy childhood and an ineffectual parent-child relationship (Apperson & McAdoo, 1968; Bene, 1965; Bieber, 1962; Brown, 1963; Evans, 1969; Freund & Blanchard, 1983; Ibrahim, 1976; O'Connor, 1964; Schofield, 1965; Stephan, 1973; Thompson, Schwartz, McCandless, & Edwards, 1973; West, 1959). Disturbed relationships with parents (i.e., smothering, seductive mothers and cold, rejecting fathers) and broken homes were thought to interfere with resolution of the Oedipal complex, thereby causing homosexuality.

The negative link between patterns of relationships in families and sexual orientation has not been substantiated in later studies (Bell, Weinberg, & Hammersmith, 1981; Bozett, 1987; Freedman, 1971; Greenblatt, 1966; Hooker, 1969; Robinson, Skeen, Flake-Hobson, & Herrman, 1982; Shavelson, Biaggio, Cross, & Lehman, 1980; Siegelman, 1974, 1981; Skeen & Robinson, 1984, 1985; Storms, 1980; Westwood, 1960). In contrast, many of these studies report positive, early parent-child relationships. Despite these recent findings, the idea that problems in the parent-child relationship causes homosexuality is commonly held in much of society and is likely to make parents' easy and guilt-free acceptance of their child's homosexuality difficult.

Except for a few unpublished reports from small samples of parents (Feinstein, 1982; King, 1980), investigations of parents' relationships with their homosexual children have been retrospective reports of homosexual children regarding these relationships. The purpose of the present study was to obtain a parental perspective regarding relationships with their homosexual children from a large sample of parents. Of particular interest were responses to the initial knowledge that their child was homosexual, the process of adjusting to the homosexuality of their child, their feelings of responsibility, and their attitudes toward the AIDS epidemic.

METHOD

Subjects

Subjects were 402 parents of gay and lesbian children, 105 fathers, and 298 mothers. They were recruited through two national organizations (302 from the Federation of Parents and Friends of Lesbians and Gays [PFLAG] and 99 from the National Federation of Parents and Friends of Gays [PFOG]). The primary purpose of these organizations is to help parents and their gay children understand one another, and to offer mutual support wherever it is needed. In addition, a snowball procedure was used in which (a) homosexual young adults were asked to supply the names and addresses of their parents (if their parents knew of their homosexuality) and (b) participants were asked to supply names and addresses of other parents they knew who have a homosexual child (children). See Table 1 for a description of the sample.

The ages of parents ranged from 37 to 82. The majority were Caucasian; blacks and Hispanics were underrepresented. Parents were well educated with most having more than a high school education. Only 24% had an annual family income of less than $20,000; most reported middle to upper level incomes. More were from the West than any other region, but the distribution by size of community was fairly even. Most considered themselves participants in organized religion, with about one-third considering themselves very religious. However, 56% reported that they only rarely or occasionally attended a religious service.

PROCEDURE

All PFOG chapter leaders received letters briefly explaining the nature of the study. A stamped, addressed envelope, and a form to request questionnaires was provided for those chapters willing to participate. Chapter leaders were asked to indicate the number of members who would participate and to return the request form within one week. A questionnaire, designed by the researchers, consent forms, and separate postage-paid envelopes for the ques-

Table 1

Distribution of Sample Characteristics

REGION OF COUNTRY		SIZE OF COMMUNITY		AGE	
Northeast	14%	< 50,000	25%	30'S	< 1%
South	25%	50,000-99,999	20%	40'S	18%
Midwest	21%	100,000-500,000	31%	50'S	42%
West	40%	> 500,00	24%	60'S	31%
				70'S	8%
				80'S	< 1%

PARENT GENDER		EDUCATION		INCOME	
Fathers	25%	Less than High School	4%	< $20,000	24%
Mothers	75%	High School Diploma	23%	$20,000-$39,999	38%
		More than High School	73%	> $40,000	38%

RACE		RELIGIOUS PREFERENCE		HOW RELIGIOUS	
White	97%	None/Other	22%	Very	37%
Other	3%	Protestant	47%	Moderate	29%
		Catholic	13%	Not at all	34%
		Jewish	18%		

GENERAL ATTITUDES		TARGET CHILD			
		AGE		GENDER	
Very Liberal	30%				
Somewhat Liberal	48%	Teens	2%	Male	71%
Somewhat Conservative	20%	20's	57%	Female	29%
Very Conservative	2%	30's	35%		
		40's	6%		

tionnaires and consent forms were mailed to each group leader who was willing to distribute the materials during a regular meeting.

Members of PFLAG received explanation letters, request forms, and postage-paid return envelopes through their regular newsletter. Both group leaders and individual parents who requested questionnaires received them through the mail. All participants were ensured anonymity; names were not associated with questionnaires. Questionnaires and signed consent forms were returned by individuals in separate postage-paid envelopes. Parents who were husband-wife couples were asked not to discuss their responses with each other until all materials had been completed and returned.

It was difficult to calculate a precise return rate because most questionnaires were distributed by second parties; it could not be determined how many of the questionnaires that were given to second parties were actually distributed. However, the number of questionnaires completed and returned compared to the number of questionnaires mailed to group leaders for possible distribution would suggest a return rate of at least 54%.

Parents who had more than one gay child (approximately 50 in this sample) were asked to report their experience with reference to only one gay child, to think of the same child when responding to each question.

Instrument

Questions were written by the authors and pretested with a group of 20 parents of homosexual children. Suggestions from this group were incorporated in the questionnaire. Suggestions from a few homosexuals and lesbians also were included. Items also were evaluated for face validity by national officers of PFLAG.

This report is based on responses to inquiries about the initial reaction to the knowledge that a child was gay, the experience of adjusting to that knowledge, feelings of responsibility for the child's homosexuality, and attitudes toward the AIDS epidemic.

Initial reaction was assessed by asking parents to circle all words in a list (or write in other words) that described the way they felt when they first learned for sure that their child was homosexual. Table 2 (found later in the article) contains the complete list of descriptions. The list was developed in consultation with homosexuals and parents of homosexuals. All of their suggestions represented negative reactions. To provide some balance, the word *glad* was added to represent a positive response and *didn't matter* and *same as usual* were added to represent neutral responses.

Parents were asked about the adjustment process they might have experienced in accepting the homosexuality of their child. One question was, "As you have responded over time to the knowledge that your child is gay, which of the following stages have you gone through?" Parents were asked to circle all that applied from the following: shock, denial, guilt, anger, and acceptance. These words have been used by Kubler-Ross (1969) to describe the emotions associated with the process of dealing with death. These parents were asked if they went through the stages in the order listed, and if they did not, to describe their own experience.

Examples of items related to feelings of responsibility for the child's homosexuality are, "Do you feel guilty because your child is gay?" and "Do you think that you caused your child to be homosexual?" Examples of items related to the AIDS epidemic are, "The AIDS outbreak has caused me to feel more negatively about homosexuals" and "The AIDS outbreak has made me more cautious of physical contact with my child." Responses were on a 4-point Likert-type scale: strongly agree to strongly disagree.

In order to construct a score representing attitudes toward AIDS, relevant AIDS items were combined. The higher the score, the more positive/constructive the response to the AIDS epidemic. A reliability estimate was calculated yielding a Cronbach alpha value of .70.

A measure of the parents' liberalism versus conservatism was obtained by asking parents to respond to the statement, "I would describe my general attitudes about how people behave as _____ _____." Responses were on a 4-point Likert-type scale: very liberal to very conservative.

Limitations

Several limitations warrant caution in interpreting these findings. Data came from parental support groups that were already formed for a common purpose. Parents of gays and lesbians who join groups and are available to participate in research have identified themselves publicly, whereas parents of homosexual children who are not members of a support group may have a different set of concerns. The high acceptance level of the parents in this study may indeed be a function of the fact that so many were participants in the support groups from which they were recruited or, perhaps, a function of their high level of education. A further limitation is the fact that almost 75% of this sample is mothers. Also the gender of child in about 70% of these reports is male. Therefore, mothers and male homosexuals are overrepresented in this sample. Nevertheless, the value of these data should not be overlooked. This was a direct assessment of parents rather than reliance on children's perceptions of parental attitudes and beliefs. Moreover, the sample size is large and all regions of the country are represented.

RESULTS

Feelings and Beliefs About Child's Homosexuality

Most parents reported having several different feelings when they first learned of their child's homosexuality. Most reported some form of regret; confusion and denial were reflected in many reports. Only a few were unaffected or angry. Although 2% said that they were glad to learn that their child was gay, these parents wrote notes indicating that it was a relief to confirm what they had suspected, not that they were glad the child was homosexual. (See Table 2.)

As many as 26% of the parents stated that they suspected their offspring's homosexuality but did not want to know for sure. However, a 72-year-old mother confessed, "I was relieved to be able to at least really know my son. At last he would be his true self. The invisible wall had finally disappeared. No more living two different lives; one for himself and one for the family he loves."

As they responded over time to knowledge that their child was gay, 64% (63% of fathers, 66% of mothers) reported that they experienced a five-stage progression of mourning and loss in dealing with their emotions: shock, denial, guilt, anger, and acceptance. One mother described her shock upon hearing the news of her child, "I was hysterical. I spent two days in bed mentally hysterical. In the past I had never retreated to bed over anything." A 66-year-old mother described the denial stage, "I thought it was not really true, that she would still meet someone from the opposite sex with whom she could have an intimate relationship." Guilt was expressed by still another 62-year-old mother, "I thought it was an illness caused

Table 2

Feelings at First Learning of Child's Homosexuality:

Percentage of Fathers and Mothers Reporting

FEELING	F* %	M %	B %	FEELING	F %	M %	B %
Afraid for child	67	77	74	Angry that child was gay	21	22	22
Sad	56	68	64	Embarrased	22	21	20
Sorry	59	57	58	Afraid for self	16	20	19
Depressed	42	52	49	Child suddenly a stranger	7	18	16
Guilty	33	48	44	Sick	5	17	14
Bewildered	36	40	39	Did not matter	7	11	10
Shocked	37	36	37	Same as usual	10	9	9
Disbelief	32	36	35	Disgust	10	8	9
Hurt	35	33	33	Angry to be told	6	3	4
Suspected, didn't know for sure	21	28	26	Glad	2	2	2

* F: Fathers
  M: Mothers
  B: Both

by something I had done wrong or failed to do that I should have done." Anger was exemplified by a 53-year-old mother who said, "I was angry that my child did not trust enough to tell me. I had to confront her." Acceptance was manifested in such comments as the 56-year-old mother who said," I was pleased he had found himself, had friends, I wanted him to know I loved him."

Many parents compared learning of their child's homosexuality to mourning an offspring's death. One 46-year-old mother, for example, remarked, "I mourned her as if she had died. Felt like she had died even though intellectually I knew she was alive." Mourning was also expressed through a mother's fear of psychological loss and separation, "I feared that I might lose him because I didn't know or understand his lifestyle. We had always been very close and shared so many of our feelings." Despite initial difficulty in dealing with knowledge of their child's sexual orientation, 97% of mothers and fathers indicated that they had worked through earlier stages and had arrived at the level of acceptance. Only 22% indicated that they still felt guilty because their child was gay. More mothers (24%) than fathers (17%) still felt guilty. (See Table 3.)

The vast majority of parents (87%) believed their children were born gay or lesbian and that their child's homosexuality was not caused by them (77%) or by their spouse (82%) (see Table 3). Only 10% believed the way the child was reared caused their child to be gay, 6% believed their child was influenced by friends who were gay, 4% attributed their children's homosexuality to the way they were treated by playmates, and 1% believed someone had convinced the child to be gay or lesbian. In general, feelings that the child was born gay were strongest if the child was male. Female children were seen as being slightly more vulnerable to the influence of others, but not more likely to be gay because of the way they were reared.

Only one person reported that the spouse was the cause of the child's sexual orientation; this person also indicated that the child had been "born that way." Evidently, it was something other than the spouse's interaction with or behavior toward the child that was considered causative in this case.

Only two reported that they believed themselves to have caused the child's homosexuality. One of these thought the child had been "born that way" and one thought it was the influence of others. Several parents indicated that occasionally they wondered if they (9%) or their spouse (5%) had caused their child's homosexuality. Others reported that they did not know if they or their spouse had caused their child's homosexuality: 13% reported that they did not know if their spouse had caused it; 14% said they did not know if they had caused it. In this sample, these were the parents who were most likely to report that the way the child was reared caused homosexuality. Two-thirds reported that they had never thought that either they or their spouse had caused their child's homosexuality.

Table 3

Parent Views on Causes of Homosexuality

Cause	Views (%)		
	Father[a]	Mother[b]	Both
Born that way	86	87	87
Way child treated	7	11	10
Influence of gay friends	8	5	6
Way treated by playmates	3	4	4
Someone convinced child	1	1	1
Don't know	14	18	17
Thinks spouse caused			
sometimes, always	2	7	6
rarely, never	89	79	81
don't know	8	14	13
Think you caused			
sometimes, always	6	10	9
rarely, never	82	74	77
don't know	11	15	14

a $_n$ = 105
b $_n$ = 298

Attitudes Toward AIDS

Responses of mothers and fathers to AIDS questions were very similar. Although only 2% of the parents said their children had developed AIDS, the majority (71%) said they worried that their children might catch AIDS. It is important to note that more parents were worried if their child was male (86%) than if their child was female (28%). Another 78% worried more about the health conditions of their children's sexual partners. Parents of lesbians were not as worried as parents of gay men, perhaps because lesbian women have the least chance of any group of contracting AIDS. Still, most parents (89%) indicated that the AIDS outbreak had not caused them to feel more negative about homosexuals, but most (61%) reported that it had not caused them to feel more positive either. Fully 98% said they admired Rock Hudson for speaking out about his AIDS. A total of 99.2% disagreed with the statement that "AIDS broke out among homosexuals as punishment for their sins."

Many parents (47%) had advised their children about the risk of AIDS. As might be expected, more parents of males (49%) had advised their child than had parents of females (23%); 31% said they would like to counsel their offspring. Few parents (3%) feared catching AIDS from their children or their friends, and, in fact, 95% rejected the statement that "If my child had AIDS, I would not go near him/her." Only 4% said that the AIDS outbreak had made them more cautious of physical contact with their child, and only two respondents said they would abandon their child if he or she had AIDS. Whereas only 15% agreed that if their child had AIDS they would keep it a secret from other family members, about half (51%) said they would keep it a secret from persons outside the family.

Parents were evenly split over the attitudes of the medical profession toward AIDS. Only 46% indicated that physicians' attitudes are appropriate. A sizeable number (38%) secretly wished that AIDS were more common among heterosexuals so their children would not be the target of so much negativism.

Parents indicated they had kept up with the progress of AIDS research (87%) but wanted to know more about AIDS (91%). Although 58% believed that media coverage on AIDS had presented a balanced attitude, 80% felt that more media coverage on AIDS is needed and 93% believed that more money for AIDS research is needed.

AIDS Attitude Scores

Nineteen of the 23 AIDS questions were employed to construct an AIDS Attitude Score. Examples of items included are "I believe AIDS broke out among homosexuals as punishment for their sins" and "If my child had AIDS I would want to keep it a secret from other family members." An example of an item not included is "Media coverage on AIDS has presented a balanced attitude towards AIDS." The summative score was computed for each subject on the 19 questions by adding the weights given for strongly agree to strongly disagree. The higher the score, the more positive the attitude. In the total sample, scores were slightly skewed toward more positive attitudes. For example, 47% scored below the midpoint of 38 (76 was the highest possible score) and 53% scored above the midpoint.

Pearson correlation coefficients were calculated to examine the relation between the AIDS Attitude Scores and nine of the parental demographic variables. No correlation was found between positive or negative AIDS scores and sex of parent. Most other correlations were not significant (parents' education, sexual orientation, size of community, church/synagogue attendance, religiosity, and income level). A significant positive correlation, however, was found for age of parent with AIDS Attitude Scores ($r = .23, p < .001$). The older the parent, the more positive the attitudes toward AIDS and the younger the parent, the more likely attitudes were to be negative. Moreover, a positive correlation was found for liberalism/conservativism and AIDS Attitudes Scores ($r = .18, p < .0005$). The more liberal the parents' views, the more positive their attitudes toward AIDS, and the more conservative their views, the more negative their attitudes. It has been suggested that the general public's views of AIDS patients varies greatly from one city to another (Squires, 1986). However, in this study an analysis of variance indicated no significant differences by region on responses to the AIDS questions ($F(3,396) = .20; p < .89$).

In general, attitudes toward this disease appeared to be as independent of feelings and beliefs about their child's homosexuality as they were of natural groupings in the sample (i.e., demographic characteristics). Neither views of who or what caused homosexuality nor feelings about their child's homosexuality were related to AIDS scores.

DISCUSSION

Initial Reactions and Grief

Despite the fact that the parents in this study were liberal and well educated, almost all of them indicated some form of negative initial reaction to learning of their child's homosexuality. The stages of grief reported by parents in this study are similar to those identified by Kubler-Ross (1969) as being associated with the knowledge of one's own impending death or loss of a loved one: denial, anger, bargaining, depression, and acceptance. The stages here are also similar to those outlined by Sauerman (1984) in a pamphlet written for gay and lesbian young adults about the process most parents go through when they learn of their child's homosexuality: shock, denial, guilt, expression of feelings, personal decision making, and true acceptance. A recent study identified six stages through which mothers progress when their children chose an "alternate" lifestyle, be it drugs, homosexuality, biracial marriage, and so on (Brans & Smith, 1987). Mothers progress through the stages of shock, attention, action, detachment, autonomy, and connection as they mourn their children and eventually learn to let go of their children and love them without grasping.

Evidence of the presence of various stages of grief among parents of homosexuals has been found in case material (Switzer & Switzer, 1980). The five stages identified in the current study, however, represent the first such large-scale systematic documentation of an ordered grief process by parents of homosexuals. According to Borhek (1983), parents of gays and lesbians mourn over the loss of an image they have carried of their children for their offsprings' lifetime. The identification of this child as a heterosexual person is demolished, and parents must grieve in order to rebuild a new identification:

The *you* they thought they knew is gone, and yet the *you* they see and deal with now seems hardly any different. This is why it may be hard for them not to hope that somehow this trauma will vanish and everything will return to the way it used to be. They need to grieve but it is difficult for them to do this when you are obviously alive and well. (Borhek, 1983, p. 61)

Although an overwhelming majority of parents in the present study had worked through their feelings of loss and arrived at the acceptance level, some (despite the benefit of a support group) had not progressed that far. They may have gotten stuck in one of the stages or regressed to an earlier stage from time to time, as a 65-year-old mother who said, "I still revert to denial." In addition, stages can occur out of order, as a 44-year-old mother reported, "Although I suspected for years, I denied it until he came out and told me. At that point, I felt shock, guilt, and anger. Gradually, these have lessened and I have been accepting ever since." Others progress through the stages in varying lengths of time, anywhere from months to years (Sauerman, 1984).

It has been suggested that it takes parents two years to work through their grief and fully accept a child's same-sex orientation (Borhek, 1983), the same amount of time expected to complete the grief process associated with a divorce or death of a family member. Still, most parents accepted and supported their children's way of life after working through their grief and learning more about homosexuality and gay and lesbian lifestyles. Some parents were gay rights activists themselves.

Findings in the present study are corroborated by those of Feinstein (1982), who found that parents' initial responses to children's homosexuality are transformed over the course of time in profound and important ways that she called "recasting the past." The evolvement of accepting parental behaviors also has been documented in case studies. "Most of the parents we have heard from or about have moved beyond their initial heartaches, fears, and doubts; they have come to see a new aspect of their gay child's life in a fresh and realistic perspective" (Fairchild & Hayward, 1979, p. 70).

Certainly the vast majority of the parents in the present study had progressed to the point of acceptance of their children. Their acceptance was evident in their comments when asked what they would tell other parents who had just learned that their child was gay. The struggle of these parents was evident from the following examples:

Love her/him, simply love her/him. Respect your child's right and wisdom to make his own choices. Affirm his honesty and courage. Celebrate his sexuality as a gift from God. (A 50-year-old mother)

They have gone through so much within themselves, just be there to listen and continue to love them. (A 52-year-old mother)

Take care, go easy, try to understand (easier said than done). (A 55-year-old father)

Your child is the same person you loved before you learned of the gayness. So don't throw away your child. (A 73-year-old mother)

Parental Perceptions of Cause

Neither psychoanalytic nor learning theory interpretations of the etiology of homosexuality were endorsed by parents in the current sample. A majority of parents did not attribute their child's homosexuality to inadequate relationships with themselves or their spouses. These views were shared by parents, studied by King (1980), who disagreed with their homosexual children that parental interactions had contributed to their offsprings' same-sex orientation. Only 10% of respondents in this study believed the way the child was reared led to his or her sexual orientation. Even fewer attributed the causes to such factors as influences of gay friends, the way the child was treated by playmates, or that someone convinced the child, although lesbian children were considered slightly more vulnerable to the influence of others. Parents overwhelmingly focused on biological rather than social factors. They believed their children were born homosexual. The importance of biological factors has also been recognized by Ruse (1981), Storms (1980), and Zuger (1976). Additional support for the importance of biological factors is found in recent research that suggests that homosexuality "clumps" in families, as when 22% of gay men had gay or bisexual brothers, compared to only 4% of heterosexual men who had gay siblings (Pillard & Weinrich, 1986).

AIDS Epidemic

Fear of the spread of AIDS, that their offspring might catch AIDS, or that their child might suffer from the backlash of AIDS were real concerns for most parents. The AIDS outbreak seemed to reopen old wounds for 90% of the parents who had come to accept their child's homosexuality after working through a series of emotions over a period of years. Now, a whole set of problems were presented to them. One 55-year-old father said, "I am concerned that some of the advances toward acceptance (of homosexuality) by the general public will be reversed and that personal danger and harassment still remain." Another 47-year-old mother echoed that concern, "It (AIDS) has made it harder to have a gay child. It's something else to worry about. It has made people less accepting of gays."

Recent findings indicate that AIDS phobia is more prevalent among hospital workers who are older, have low contact with AIDS patients, and who have homophobic attitudes (Pleck, O'Donnell, O'Donnell, & Snarey, 1988). Contrary to these findings, parents in the present study did not feel more negatively about homosexuality because of AIDS. They did, however, report a resurgence of fear surrounding their child's sexual orientation. Not only did they worry that their child might catch AIDS, but worried about the health condition of their child's sexual partners. Still, they did not fear physical contact with their children and thoughts of abandoning, rejecting, or shunning their offspring in the event of AIDS was unthinkable. Apparently, even though parents are concerned about the AIDS outbreak and worry that their child might catch AIDS, the spread of the disease has not altered their feelings toward their children or their views of homosexuality in general.

When asked if the spread of AIDS had affected their attitudes toward homosexuality, some took the opportunity to point out that homosexual behavior should not be confused with the state of being homosexual. Many others reported that AIDS is not caused by ho-

mosexuality; it is disease that is spread via promiscuity, not homosexuality. Many expressed disapproval of promiscuity, but were
careful to distinguish it from homosexuality.

But the tragedy of AIDS has had a more profound effect on parents of homosexual children than on most other groups. The social
stigma of having a gay child was reported as being difficult, and the
threat of AIDS has clearly intensified the concerns of these parents,
as the following examples illustrate:

> It breaks my heart they have one more thing to be burdened
> with. (A 46-year-old mother)

> It brings out negative feelings about homosexuality and may
> cause a backlash and less understanding of homosexuality. (A
> 55-year-old mother)

> I feel very good that I supported my son for being himself all
> during his life. That has made his death much easier to accept.
> I wouldn't have traded him for 50 heterosexual sons. He en-
> riched the lives of most everyone who would allow it. (A 59-
> year-old mother)

For these parents, the experience of having a gay child has not
been easy. Many continue to struggle to gain acceptance for themselves. Such feelings were expressed well by one mother:

> I do not want pity from anyone because I have a gay child. I
> just want them to understand me. Don't look down on me
> when I go to a meeting and have people say, "Oh, there is
> Mrs. Smith. Oh, isn't it too bad she has a gay child." I want
> them to say, "Oh, there is Mrs. Smith. How nice it is that she
> is at the meeting."

IMPLICATIONS FOR RESEARCHERS

Studies of families with one or more gay members should be
designed with the same guidelines as other studies of families. For
example, samples should be representative and multiple methods
should be used. However, concern over these issues should not

result in no studies of families with gay members. As more studies of such families are published, it will become easier to reach potential subjects, thereby improving the quality of subsequent research. In the meantime, every effort should be made to understand the kinds of biases that are embedded in the samples we can obtain, and those biases should be considered carefully as data are interpreted.

Perhaps most important is the need for studies of whole families. Homosexual children and parents should be studied from the same families. Likewise, the siblings and other close family members should be included. Multigenerational studies are of particular interest given that there is reason to believe that more than one generation in the same family is likely to have homosexual members.

IMPLICATIONS FOR HELPING PROFESSIONALS

More than twice as many mothers as fathers participated in this study. It is also true that more mothers than fathers participate in support groups; thus, it may be true that most fathers are not being reached. Professionals may need to consider innovative ways of reaching men who can be expected to need support just as do women. Knowing of the initial difficulties expressed by parents in this survey leads one to conclude that parents who do not have the advantage of a support group may be having a much harder time adjusting to news of their child's homosexuality as well as to the AIDS epidemic. Because of AIDS, support groups for parents of homosexuals are more essential today than ever before. Not only do they assist parents in working through their feelings concerning dealing with a child's homosexuality, but they also help parents cope with fears about AIDS. More specialized services are needed to meet the needs of all family members, siblings, and grandparents, as well as parents in coming to terms with understanding and accepting the homosexuality of a family member.

Additionally, professionals must also make a concerted effort to provide information for the public via various media. Fellow professionals and those who shape public policy also must be educated.

CONCLUSION

The overall high acceptance level of the parents in this study may indeed be a function of their participation in the support group from which they were recruited. Still, the road to acceptance of a homosexual child was a long, painful, and difficult one for most parents. Also, fear of the spread of AIDS, that their offspring might catch AIDS, or that their child might suffer from the backlash of AIDS, were real concerns for most parents. Despite these concerns, the spread of AIDS had not altered their feelings toward their children or their views of homosexuality in general. One mother summed up the feelings of many: "I feel more compassion for the men that are dying. It could be my child. I hope the media doesn't just show the negative side but educates that these are human beings as are we all."

REFERENCES

Apperson, L. B., & McAdoo, W. G. (1968). Parental factors in the childhood of homosexuals. *Journal of Abnormal Psychology, 73*, 201-206.

Bell, A. P., Weinberg, M.S., & Hammersmith, S. K. (1981). *Sexual preference: Its development in men and women*. Bloomington, IN: Indiana University Press.

Bene, E. (1965). On the genesis of male homosexuality: An attempt at clarifying the role of the parents. *British Journal of Psychiatry, 111*, 803-813.

Bozett, F. (1987). *Gay and lesbian parents*. New York: Praeger.

Bieber, I. (1962). *Homosexuality: A psychoanalytic study*. New York: Basic Books.

Borhek, M. V. (1983). *Coming out to parents; A two-way survival guide for lesbians and gay men and their parents*. New York: Pilgrim Press.

Brans, J., & Smith, M. T. (1987). *Mother, I have something to tell you*. New York: Doubleday.

Brown, D. G. (1963). Homosexuality and family dynamics. *Bulletin of the Menninger Clinic, 27*, 227-232.

Evans, R. B. (1969). Childhood parental relationships of homosexual men. *Journal of Consulting and Clinical Psychology, 33*, 129-135.

Fairchild, B., & Hayward, N. (1979). *Now that you know: What every parent should know about homosexuality*. New York: Harcourt Brace Jovanovich.

Feinstein, N. J. (1982). *Caught in the middle: Parental response to their adult children's homosexuality*. Unpublished doctoral dissertation, The Wright Institute, Berkeley, CA.

Freedman, M. (1971). *Homosexuality and psychological functioning.* Belmont, CA: Brooks/Cole.

Freund, K., & Blanchard, R. (1983). Is the distant relationship of fathers and homosexual sons related to the sons' erotic preference for male partners, or to the sons' atypical gender identity, or to both? *Journal of Homosexuality, 9*(3), 7-25.

Greenblatt, D. (1966). *Semantic differential analysis of the "Triangular System" hypothesis in "adjusted" male homosexuals.* Unpublished doctoral dissertation, University of California, Los Angeles.

Hooker, E. (1969). Parental relations and male homosexuality in patient and non-patient samples. *Journal of Consulting and Clinical Psychology, 33,* 140-142.

Ibrahim, A. (1976). The home situation and the homosexual. *Journal of Sex Research, 12,* 263-282.

King, W. M. (1980). *The etiology of homosexuality as related to childhood experiences and adult adjustment: A study of the perceptions of homosexual males, their parents, and siblings.* Unpublished doctoral dissertation, Indiana University, Bloomington, IN.

Kubler-Ross, E. (1969). *On death and dying.* New York: Macmillan.

O'Connor, P. J. (1964). Aetiological factors in homosexuality as seen in Royal Air Force psychiatric practice. *British Journal of Psychiatry, 110,* 381-391.

Pillard, A., & Weinrich, J. (1986). Gays: A family phenomenon? *Archives of General Psychiatry, 43,* 808-812.

Pleck, J. H., O'Donnell, L., O'Donnell, C., & Snarey, J. (1988). AIDS-phobia, contact with AIDS, and AIDS-related job stress in hospital workers. *Journal of Homosexuality, 15*(3/4), 41-54.

Robinson, B. E., Skeen, P., Flake-Hobson, C., & Herrman, M. (1982). Gays' perceptions of early family life: A nationwide pilot study. *Family Relations, 31,* 79-83.

Ruse, M. (1981). Are there gay genes? Sociobiology and homosexuality. *Journal of Homosexuality, 6*(4), 5-34.

Sauerman, T. H. (1984). *Coming out to your parents.* Los Angeles, CA: Federation of Parents & Friends of Lesbians and Gays.

Schofield, M. (1965). *Sociological aspects of homosexuality.* Boston: Little, Brown.

Shavelson, E., Biaggio, M. K., Cross, H. H., & Lehman, R. E. (1980). Lesbian women's perceptions of their parent-child relationships. *Journal of Homosexuality, 5,* 205-215.

Siegelman, M. (1974). Parental background of homosexuals and heterosexuals. *Archives of Sexual Behavior, 3,* 3-18.

Siegelman, M. (1981). Parental backgrounds of homosexual and heterosexual men: A cross national replication. *Archives of Sexual Behavior, 10,* 505-513.

Skeen, P., & Robinson, B. E. (1984). Family backgrounds of gay fathers: A descriptive study. *Psychological Reports, 54,* 999-1005.

Skeen, P., & Robinson, B. E. (1985). Gay fathers' and gay nonfathers' relationship with their parents. *Journal of Sex Research, 21,* 86-91.

Squires, S. (1986, September). Psychologists discuss effects of AIDS at annual conference. *The Charlotte Observer*, p. 25A.

Stephan, W. G. (1973). Parental relationships and early social experiences of activist male homosexuals and male heterosexuals. *Journal of Abnormal Psychology, 82*, 506-513.

Storms, M. D. (1980). Theories of sexual orientation. *Journal of Personality and Social Psychology, 38*, 783-792.

Switzer, D. K., & Switzer, S. (1980). *Parents of the homosexual*. Philadelphia: Westminster Press.

Tompson, N. L., Schwartz, D. M., McCandless, B. R., & Edwards, D. A. (1973). Parent-child relationships and sexual identity in male and female homosexuals and heterosexuals. *Journal of Consulting and Clinical Psychology, 41*, 120-127.

West, D. J. (1959). Parental figures in the genesis of male homosexuality. *International Journal of Social Psychiatry, 5*, 85-97.

Westwood, G. (1960). *A minority*. London: Longmans.

Woodman, N. J. (1985). Parents of lesbians and gays: Concerns and intervention. In H. Hidalgo, T. L. Peterson, & N. J. Woodman (Eds.), *Lesbian and gay issues: A resource manual for social workers* (pp. 21-32). Silver Springs, MD: National Association of Social Workers.

Zuger, B. (1976). Monozygotic twins discordant for homosexuality: Report of a pair and significance of the phenomenon. *Comprehensive Psychiatry, 17*, 661-670.

Heterosexual Women's Perceptions of Their Marriages to Bisexual or Homosexual Men

Dorothea Hays, EdD, RN, CS

Adelphi University

Aurele Samuels, BA

University of Pennsylvania

SUMMARY. Twenty-one heterosexual women who were or had been married to bisexual or homosexual men and had children by them responded to a 28-page questionnaire that explored their experiences as wives and mothers. All of the married women expected a lasting, monogamous marriage. Only three had partial knowledge of their husband's sexual orientation before marriage. All of them went through a painful grief reaction when they learned that their husbands had emotional or sexual, or both, attachments to other men. The suffering was aggravated by feeling deceived or stupid for not having guessed the truth. What made it difficult for them to seek support from family and friends was the fear of encountering social disapproval or ostracism. They were afraid for themselves, their husbands, and their children. At the time of the study 11 of the 21

Dr. Hays is Professor at Adelphi University, Marion A. Buckley School of Nursing. Aurele Samuels is a graduate student at the University of Pennsylvania School of Social Work.

The authors wish to acknowledge the contributions of the many people who helped in the construction, validation, and revisions of the questionnaire used for this study. They wish to give special thanks to Dr. Frederick Bozett, Dr. Alice Fennessey, Dr. Clarence Tripp, Dr. Jean Gochros, Dr. David Matteson, and Dr. Timothy Wolf.

Correspondence and reprint requests may be addressed to the authors, c/o Adelphi University, Marion A. Buckley School of Nursing, Garden City, NY 11530.

81

women were still married and living with their husbands, but most of them felt unsure that the marriage would last. Ten were in transition, separated, or divorced. Only three of the still married wives had complete confidence in the future stability of their relationships. These marriages were characterized by good communications, husbands who considered themselves bisexual, and an open marriage contract whereby wives could have heterosexual affairs. Findings cannot be generalized from this small convenience sample, but will hopefully encourage further research. The writers are also soliciting more subjects to enlarge the sample.

According to Kinsey, Pomeroy, Martin, and Gebhard, whose famous study appeared in 1948, "data make it appear probable that the true incidence of the homosexual in married groups is much higher than we are able to record" (p. 289).

Homosexuality and bisexuality are no longer considered an illness and are becoming more and more acceptable orientations. However, the disclosure process is still painful and often socially undesirable for many men. Ignorance and stigma attached to homosexuality remain widespread. Many women have entered into marriages to homosexual or bisexual men with insufficient knowledge of the facts and the possible consequences to themselves and their children. Although extensive research is available to describe and examine male homosexuals, little is known about their wives. Women who learn that their husbands are actively homosexual are often too ashamed to seek help or let others know about their problems.

Self-help groups for such wives are beginning to offer the opportunity to exchange information and to give and receive support. Attending such a group made the authors aware of the need to systematically to collect information about and for these women.

This research study was designed to examine the experiences of heterosexual women who are or have been married to homosexual men and have had children by them. The focus is on women with children because having children constitutes a strong commitment to marriage. Moreover, concerns for the children's welfare cause additional stress for parents when the marriage fails or is not socially sanctioned.

The purpose of this study was to collect data leading to the formulation of hypotheses that can be tested later with matched control groups. The researchers were interested in the following areas:

1. Why do women enter heterogeneous marriages (heterosexual women married to bisexual or homosexual men) and are there any special characteristics that differentiate these women from those who marry heterosexual men?
2. How do wives' experiences of such marriages differ during each stage, beginning with courtship, from experiences of wives married to heterosexual men?
3. Why do some women stay in heterogeneous marriages and others do not?
4. How do wives and children deal with the experiences and problems of disclosure, social stigma, and homosexual activities of the husband/father?
5. What special concerns do these mothers have for their children?
6. Are there differences in wives' experiences of the marriage based on the information provided or withheld before marriage about the husband's sexual orientation and activity?
7. Do these wives experience major crises and what factors precipitate them?
8. To whom do they turn for help?

The literature provides mixed information about the characteristics of women who marry homosexual or bisexual men. Myra Hatterer (1974) treated five wives of homosexual husbands who were in therapy to change their sexual orientation, and she interviewed 12 additional wives. She found that these women all had had psychosexual problems before marriage, including feeling inadequate in heterosexual relationships and doubting their own attractiveness. They had conflicts in their relationships with their fathers, and some had competed unsuccessfully for their fathers' attention with their brothers. Most had searched for undemanding sexual relations. After marriage they felt trapped and reacted with hostility to their husbands' sexual inadequacy.

Hatterer discovered that these women were reluctant to change the dynamics of their marriages, therefore hindering their husbands' efforts to change. They were also afraid to enter therapy and to examine an unsatisfactory marriage that might include the consideration of dissolution. These data were collected during or after these women experienced the stress of living with homosexual spouses.

Wolf (1982) studied 36 couples in stable heterosexual marriages in which homosexual expression by the husband was coexistent. He described the women as "a unique set of individuals with few obvious characteristics in common" (p. 107). But he did find that "they had made crucial compromises in order to sustain their marriages" (p. 107). The compromises were in the area of sexual fulfillment. The women valued their good friendships with their husbands which they received in return. Wolf found 60% of the women in his sample were firstborn, and those who were not had many characteristics of firstborns, such as high performance goals and problems with anxiety.

Nahas and Turley (1979) also found no common personality profile for the women involved in relationships with gay men. They divided their study population into traditional couples, marginal relationships, and new couples. They found that "few of the traditional-couple women had a complete understanding of homosexuality; some thought it was a phase that could be 'cured' in therapy" (p. 277). The women in marginal friendships appreciated gay men's "understanding of and sensitivity to women" (p. 279). The women among new couples "generally felt good about themselves and had no illusions about the man's eventually altering his homosexuality" (p. 279). Most heterogeneous marriages end in divorce after disclosure of homosexuality to the wife (Bozett, 1982). Why do some women stay married to bisexual or homosexual men?

Malone (1980), who interviewed more than 150 men and women, found that some women felt they could save the men from homosexuality, others did not realize their lover was gay, and "a few women fall in love with a series of homosexual men out of some personal neurosis" (p. 7). Nahas and Turley (1979) found that women liked gay men because they were "comfortable, stimulating companions" (p. 124) who seem to understand women and their problems.

Malone (1980) found that sexual relationships between heterosexual women and gay men were problematic but quite common, and thought they offered each other "companionship, sympathetic understanding, moral support, and increased self-awareness" (p. 15). Wolf (1982) found that the couples he studied "were sexually attracted to one another, maintained sexual activity, and expressed satisfaction about this activity" (p. 99).

Although some studies emphasized the wife's role in helping her husband to become heterosexual, they also indicated the husband's tendency to blame her for not being more successful (Hatterer, 1970; Sanders, 1980). Others discussed the almost inevitable reversion of the husband to homosexual activity and the increasing aversion or indifference toward sex with his wife (Bell & Weinberg, 1978: Humphreys & Miller, 1980; Karlen, 1980; West, 1977).

How do the wives deal with the various problems they encounter because of their husbands' sexual orientation? Tripp (1976) stated:

> The patient's marriage to a partner he cares about is considered the major breakthrough. (How interesting it is, and how alarming, that the risks and comforts of the spouse are never mentioned; the massive literature on how to alter homosexuality contains not a word on his or her behalf.) (p. 238)

Gochros (1982, 1985) studied the reactions of 33 wives to their husband's coming out. She found the major factor to be the content and context of the disclosure of homosexuality, including how the wife learned about it, what was told, and how committed the husband remained. Other important factors were unrelated stress and available support systems. It was more of a crisis if the wife experienced isolation, stigma, confusion, and loss, and was without a support system to provide her with accurate information and guidance. If the husband remained committed and empathic to his wife, coming out was only a minor crisis.

Wolf (1982) found that women with more education and higher economic status also had more satisfaction in their relationships. "The crucial theme of these variables appeared to be independence of the women in these relationships" (p. 109). Their relationships with gay husbands were rated more positive if wives had sexual relationships outside their marriage. Important factors in maintaining good marital relationships were early and open communications and frequent sexual intercourse. Also important as a primary reason for staying in the relationship was friendship rather than financial security or children. In his study, 27% of the couples separated for 1 to 6 months during the process of dealing with the issue of homosexuality of the husband.

According to Wolf (1982), "The husband must be the primary support for the wife after the disclosure of his homosexual behavior and not vice versa" (p. 112). He felt that it is the therapist's duty to prepare the husband for this role. Subsequent to the husband's disclosure, Wolf advocated conjoint as well as individual therapy. The focus should be on open communication, understanding the husband's homosexual orientation, enhancing the sexual relationship, and developing support inside and outside of the marriage. The wife also needs help in developing "assertive relationships and activities which compensate for the marriage" (p. 113). It is also important for her to feel good about herself and her relationships. Wolf indicated that five years may be a realistic time frame for acceptance and resolution of all these issues involved in a heterogeneous marriage.

Little is known about raising children in heterogeneous marriages. Lawrence Hatterer (1970) and Myra Hatterer (1974) both emphasized the paucity of research that deals with the marriages of homosexuals, their wives, and their children. While there is literature on gay fathers, nothing is known about the mothers' concerns about raising their children. Voeller (1980) stated:

> Many people date, marry, and become parents, only to realize too late the error they made. They then find themselves deeply pained, fearful of losing their children through court suits, of losing spouses they care for but are illsuited to, of depriving their spouses and themselves of more deeply appropriate and meaningful relationships, and of causing their friends and other relatives deep pain. (p. 240)

Lawrence Hatterer (1970) discussed the problems and fears of homosexual fathers, especially in raising their sons. They often try harder to be a companion and provide masculine activities. However, any criticism of his father role by his family could upset him to the point of provoking a relapse to homosexuality (p. 345). Gay fathers organizations give advice to fathers on raising their children (Gay Fathers of Toronto, 1981). Gardner (1977) discussed when and how to tell children about their father's homosexuality in his *Parents Book About Divorce*.

Wolf (1982) stated "little is known about the adaptation of children in these marriages" (p. 120). He felt that research was needed about the relationships of these children with their parents, about aspects of peer approval or disapproval, and about the children's psychosexual development. Miller (1986) found that "typically only older children (if any) are told" about their father's homosexuality for fear that it become too widely known in the community (p. 237). Bozett (1988) outlined a conceptual framework to explain methods of social control used by children to protect their own identity from societal stigma connected with their father's homosexuality.

THE STUDY

Method

The present study is unique because it specifically sought the perceptions and feelings of heterosexual women who married and had children by bisexual or homosexual men.

A questionnaire was developed based on questions raised in the literature and by women in such marriages. Portions of it were adapted with permission from Timothy Wolf's doctoral dissertation (1982). It was revised after review by six researchers in the field of homogeneous marriages and a pilot test using three subjects.

Examples of questions about entering and remaining in such marriages are "What qualities of your husband initially attracted you?" and "What factors influenced or might influence your decision to separate from your husband?" Examples of questions about experiences of wives and children are "What were the steps and stages you progressed through after his disclosure?" and "For each child describe his/her reaction when told and give your reason for not telling about the father's sexual orientation." Examples of questions about coping with stressful experiences are "Did any factors make your reactions more positive?" and "Outside of therapy, who have you found helpful in supporting you in dealing with the sexual issues and related concerns in your family relationships?"

Demographic Data

Subjects were recruited through support groups in New York, Boston, Philadelphia, Washington, and from networks of the researchers. Twenty-one subjects responded in great detail to an in-depth, 27-page questionnaire. All but four included their addresses and consent to participate in follow-up studies. Many of the women emphasized the wish for more knowledge in this area, and three stated the questionnaire was the first real help they had gotten.

The women ranged in age from 32 to 62 years, with a mean age of 47.7 years. They had been married from 6 to 37 years, with a median of 18 years and a mean of 19.57 years. Over half of them (11) were still married and living with their bisexual or homosexual husbands, but only three felt sure that their marriages would be long-lived. Six of those still married felt they had significantly compromised their values and beliefs about primary relationships in order to remain in the marriage.

Nearly half of the subjects (10) were not living with their husbands. Five of them were legally separated and one was married to a heterosexual man.

Fourteen of the husbands considered themselves homosexual, five bisexual, one heterosexual (although he had male lovers), and one would not discuss it with his wife.

Subjects' educational levels ranged from high school to PhD and MD, with 42% having graduate degrees. They came from all walks of life. There were four housewives, three secretaries, two teachers, two nurses, two administrators, and one each student, social worker, psychologist, physician, potter, university professor, and computer programmer, and one who did not specify. Incomes ranged from total dependence on their husbands (5), to over $100,000 income of their own (2).

Subjects' religions were Roman Catholic (4), Jewish (9), Protestant (5), Atheist (1), and "searching" (2). Five specified they were devout or seriously involved in their religions and the other 16 felt casually or not at all involved.

Similar to Wolf's (1982) findings, the majority (9) were the oldest children in their families of origin. Six were middle children, three youngest, two were only children, and one was a twin.

Most of the women (18) did not know that their husbands were bisexual or homosexual before marriage. The other three either did not understand what it meant or believed their husbands would abstain after they married. One actively homosexual husband told his wife that he was a latent homosexual. Another husband informed his wife he had had homosexual experiences only during adolescence, which was true. Six of the 18 husbands, who did not tell their wives, were aware of their bisexuality or homosexuality prior to marriage. Another six husbands discovered their homosexuality after marriage, and the remaining six never told their wives when they learned about their sexual orientation.

For future comparison studies and for primary prevention it is important to know if any of the women had experienced deprivation or abuse as children. Four reported sexual abuse, two by their fathers and two by other men. Two others were physically abused by their fathers, and three felt emotionally harassed. Four suffered prolonged absence of their fathers from their home and were sometimes overprotected by their mothers. One subject felt emotional withdrawal by both parents, one felt withdrawal only by her father, and one felt her mother to be overprotective. Only 5 out of the 21 subjects reported a childhood free of trauma.

Almost half (9) of the women did not feel they were raised with rigid values regarding sexual activity. The other 12 stated various taboos, such as "sex is allowed in marriage only" (8), "sex is not to be discussed" (2), "nice girls don't" (1), and "sex is unpleasant" (1). Nineteen subjects thought of themselves as attractive to heterosexual men before marriage; the other two were not sure.

Findings

Responses to the survey were analyzed to learn: (a) why did these marriages start and how were they experienced by the wives in the beginning?; (b) how did the wives find out about their husband's sexual orientation?; (c) how did they experience and cope with the information and resulting awareness of their husbands' homosexual activities?; (d) what were the mothers' perceptions of their children's experiences and problems with their fathers' sexual orientation?; and (e) what was unique in the marriages of those women who thought their marriages would last, with the full knowledge of their husbands' orientation?

The Beginning of Marriage

It was the first marriage for all couples. Twelve of the wives were sexually active prior to marriage. They reported sexual relationships with one to 30 heterosexual partners for periods of a few weeks to 2 years. The other nine women had had no previous sexual experience. None of them had had a relationship with a homosexual man prior to marriage.

What attracted the women to bisexual or homosexual men, and did they perceive differences in these men that might have alerted them to their sexual orientation? Subjects listed many qualities in their husband that had attracted them, such as sensitivity (6), kindness, caring, and compassion (9), good looks and sex appeal (5), intelligence (4), good sense of humor (3), aggressive, leadership and macho qualities (3), creativity (1), and support of women's rights (1).

In comparing their husband with heterosexual partners, over half (12) of the subjects saw no differences in their husband's attractive qualities. The other nine subjects mentioned greater sensitivity (3), less macho or more feminine qualities (2), greater ability to listen (1), greater ability to turn her on (1), coming on less strong (1), and being less demanding (1). All but one of the women married because they were in love. The one who did not was pressed into marriage by her family and is now divorced. Only four mentioned social or family pressures as a contributing factor. None married to cure his homosexuality.

Five subjects lived together before marriage and 14 had premarital sex with their husbands for periods of 3 months to 6 years and reported sex as mainly satisfying to extremely satisfying (10), as fair (2), and disappointing or rarely satisfying (2).

The researchers wondered how many of the women would have married knowing their husband's sexual orientation. Ten of the 18 women who did not know before marriage said "no" and the other eight checked "not sure." We also asked if they would have married if they had known all that they know now. Three said "yes" or "probably yes," 13 said "no," and five were not sure.

Were there signs in the marriage from which wives might have guessed their husbands' homosexual involvement? After being married but before disclosure the wives' main complaint was lack of communication (7), sexual deprivation (6), his mood swings (3), physical withdrawal (2), superficiality (2), and rejection and a-buse (1).

Disclosure

How did the women learn about their husbands' orientation and how did they cope with this disclosure and the changes that followed in their marriages? Three of the subjects had some knowledge of their husbands' sexual orientation before marriage. The other 18 wives were told or learned about his homosexual activities anywhere from 1.5 to 33 years after they got married, with a mean of 15.94 years and a mode of 19 years. The revelation did not come as a total surprise to most of them. Their suspicions before the actual disclosure had been raised by the decrease in the husband's sexual activity with them and his unwillingness to discuss sexual concerns, by his emotional and physical withdrawal, and by his mood swings directed toward the wives. However, eight of the women had been concerned that their husband might be having a heterosexual affair, and only five had noticed his attraction to men. The remaining five wives held no suspicions. Several women suspected homosexuality and asked their husbands outright, only to be rebuffed and ridiculed for asking such a ridiculous question.

Disclosures came in many different forms. Twelve of the wives were told by their husbands directly. For some this occurred after a separation due to a business trip. One husband told after having stayed out late repeatedly. One husband told after suspecting that his wife might have caught a venereal disease from him. Another husband told after his hospitalization for a suicide attempt. Four women learned about it in therapy, and one of them was informed only after she had an emotional breakdown. One learned by accident that her husband was going to a Gay Fathers Forum, and another noticed and commented on her husband's close friendship with a younger man.

Examples of what husbands told their wives included having an affair with a male lover, having a few homosexual experiences while away and feeling guilty, and having been attracted to men since childhood but thinking it would go away. Right after disclosure only one man wanted a divorce immediately; the others hoped for their marriages to continue.

The wives' reactions to the disclosure varied. Some experienced relief in getting validation of what was suspected together with assurance that the marriage could be worked on. Others experienced confusion, hurt, jealousy, anger, grief, disgust, and repulsion. Examples are: "I accepted it as part of his personality"; "I was relieved it was not my fault, he loved me and wanted to stay"; "I was not crazy in my suspicion"; "I was concerned about his excessive guilt, pleased at his honesty, anxious, but optimistic"; "I reacted with upset, fury and rage. I had been asking questions for 10 years, hearing rumors, all had been denied"; "I was mentally denying, refusing to accept what I did not understand, became defensive of homosexuality and myself, and refused to accept his rejection of me"; "I started to return his aggressive behaviors"; "I reacted with rage that I had spent 30 years struggling, so often alone with children, plumbing, finances, to enable him to spend whatever time he needed on his job, only to find out that he was cruising"; "I accepted his statements, cried, was grief stricken. I was six months pregnant with our first child"; "I reacted with disgust, repulsion, disbelief, nausea, and vomiting." Fourteen of the 18 wives who had not been informed before marriage reacted with extreme shock and emotional upheaval.

Most women recognized and described stages they went through following the disclosure. For some (8) there was greater closeness at first, a wish to comfort their husband and work on the marriage. Strong feelings of anger and grief came later, usually when wives found out that their husbands had lovers with whom they were not only sexually but also emotionally involved. For some that was like going through the grief process all over again, with shock and disbelief, feeling as if the men they knew had died. There was anger, despair, depression, self-doubt, loss of self-esteem. Finally, they arrived at acceptance of the facts and an attempt to make a new life for themselves, or to adjust within the marriage.

The following are examples of how subjects described this process: "I joined a women's support group and tried to accept it and make my marriage work"; "I have mellowed with time and have adjusted to a partial married relationship, mostly parenting"; "I went again through the same feelings, but more intense, because I knew for sure that he was gay, I was more upset when I realized my marriage was over"; "I was devastated. Disbelief, feelings of deep despair, self-accusation. Finally, I learned to accept what is and feel better about myself."

The wives were asked about specific emotional and physical reactions to the disclosure. All except one wife (who only felt sorry for her husband), experienced anger immediately after the disclosure. Sixteen felt depressed when the facts really sank in, and they also experienced loneliness and the uncertainty of the future of their marriage. Twelve had physical reactions, such as loss of appetite, weight gain, or headaches. One wife was constantly ill and needed hospitalization and another's heart problems worsened. Guilt was experienced by six. They blamed themselves for not having seen the cause of their husbands' strange behavior, or for not having been a better wife.

Fear was another overwhelming experience for 17 wives. The greatest fear was that the husband would abandon the family and that the future was uncertain. Only three women mentioned fear of AIDS and other genitally transmitted diseases. Twelve wives described the experience of shame. They did not want to tell anyone about their discovery. They felt different, stigmatized, and wondered what people would think of them and their marital choice.

Would it have been better if the husband had been unfaithful to them with another woman? Five said no, "I resent any infidelity"; "an affair is an affair." Eight would have preferred it, because they "might have had a fighting chance"; "His manhood would not have been the issue"; "I could have worked on it." Six would have felt worse, "I would have felt it was due to my inadequacy"; "She would have been in direct competition with me." Two did not answer.

Subjects were asked if there was any change in the quality of their relationship with their husband following the disclosure. Five women noticed abrupt changes, one toward honesty and a better sex life, one toward relief after she told him she was divorcing him, and the others negatively toward lack of trust. Gradual changes in the relationship were noted by all others. Three experienced greater truthfulness and closeness, and 10 wives felt a gradual emotional separation. One stated "It was better at first, and declined over the past two years"; another, "I learned to be more independent."

The women were asked how they rated the quality of their present relationship with their husbands. The ratings were very different for those wives who were still living with their husbands and those who were not. Wives living with their husbands checked the relationship as "outstanding" (2), "better than most" (4), "average" (1), "below average" (3), and "poor" (1). Wives not living with their husbands checked their relationship as "better than most" (1), "average" (3), "below average" (1), "poor" (4), and "no relationship except adversarily" (1).

Did their sex life change after disclosure? Six wives reported that there was no change in their own sexual satisfaction and two felt an improvement. The other 10 felt either a sudden or a gradual decrease in their sexual satisfaction. They stated: "I wanted to get away from him"; "I found it harder to respond"; "I wanted more satisfaction, but the reverse happened"; "I was afraid of AIDS"; "I felt like he was doing me a favor. I don't react as well as I used to"; "I believe he merely was doing everything by rote."

One way to cope with sexual deprivation in the marriage is to seek satisfaction outside of it. After disclosure, about half (10) of the wives had sexual relations with other men, all heterosexual. Seven did so with the encouragement of their husbands. Nine of these 10 reported great positive differences between their sexual experience with heterosexual men and their husbands, such as "much more satisfying, made me feel like a woman"; "Much more passionate, prolonged, total involvement."

Five women reported negative reactions toward their husbands' encouragement to have an affair. They felt it was done only to "get the monkey off his back," that he really did not care about the wife's feelings, and that it was generally said in anger. These feelings served to erode further the marital relationship.

Disclosure to Others

After the wives learned about their husbands' true sexual orientation, they had to make a decision about disclosure to others. Six women told their parents, the others did not; nine wives told other family members; all but three women confided in straight friends; four disclosed to gay friends; only one told her employer; four told colleagues; 17 had therapists to confide in; six told clergy; seven confided in similar couples or support groups, and one added to the checklist that she told her physician. The women gave their reasons for not telling certain people. Parents and other older relatives were not told because it would cause them too much pain and worry. It also might strain the relationship between relatives and the bisexual or homosexual husband. Some people were not told because they were known to be homophobic. One subject described her husband's reaction as outraged after she told her coworker because it created a strained relationship. She promised not to "tell another soul" but now feels ambivalent about that.

The responses of those persons in whom the wives confided were generally very supportive, and the subjects felt relief being able to tell. One woman stated: "I had to keep on talking about this to almost everyone to a point of acceptance." Other reactions were "I feared losing friends, his job, but needed to take that chance. I felt relief." "I had verbal diarrhea, told everyone." "Only after divorce I told friends. Some continue as his friends, some as mine." Telling others did not have the feared dire consequences, but the women also used discretion in their choice of confidants.

Children's Reactions

Most of the mothers were very concerned about the welfare of their children and how they might be affected by their fathers' sexual orientation. Most (15) mothers reported that some or all of their children had been told about their fathers' homosexuality. The others felt their children were too young to know, or they could not bring themselves to tell, or persuade their husbands to do so.

Some children were told by their fathers, others by their mothers, and some by both. Most of the children were upset at first, but later tried to be supportive to both parents. Several children were reported to have guessed the truth and felt relieved to get validation.

With some of the children, the parents waited too long before telling them, so that they found out from others in a more stressful way. One daughter was told by a friend in college in an insulting way. She then asked her father who confirmed the truth. One mother told her son and daughter after their father had taken them to a gay beach, an experience that confused and frightened them.

Five mothers reported that their children experienced embarrassing situations or trauma because of their fathers' sexual orientation, such as physical or verbal abuse by other children. One suffered a "mock faggot trial" at school. A friend passed on gossip to one daughter that her father had "come on" to her own boyfriend, which was not true.

Eight mothers reported that their children had met their fathers' sexual partners (five without knowing it). One mother reported that the children felt positive about it; others did not know (5); the other two reported negative reactions. All but two mothers felt uncomfortable, disgusted, and angry about their children meeting their fathers' gay lovers. They wanted to have input about the circumstances of these meetings.

The 12 mothers of older children were asked if they thought their children had problems in relationships with members of the opposite sex that might be related to their fathers' sexual orientation. Four thought so. "She had early sex to prove her femininity." "Two (out of three) daughters have difficulty finding boyfriends." "She had sexual problems first, thought wrongly to be related to homosexuality." "A guy my daughter was dating told her he 'hated fags'." "My daughter told her boyfriend that if they got married and he told her twenty years later that he was gay, she would kill him."

Five mothers answered "yes" to the question if they thought there were beneficial aspects for the children in having a bisexual or homosexual father. These mothers felt that it may make the children more tolerant toward differences in people and increase their sensitivity and understanding. Though one mother was not sure, 12 others said "no." The negative responses included an emphatic "absolutely not" and "there are too many emotional liabilities."

Mothers expressed warnings of varying intensity when asked what advice they would give a daughter considering marriage to a bisexual or homosexual man. "Think it through very carefully"; "Get clear about what you want and what your limits are"; "One must be prepared to share and undergo the pain that occurs when the husband has a lover"; "It has been too difficult for me, so please don't do it"; "What, are you crazy! Have you not suffered enough from your father because of it?"; "Absolutely not, forget it."

The mothers were emphatically opposed to their daughters marrying a homosexual or bisexual man. Less than half (9), however, checked "1" on a scale of 1 to 5, with 1 the most important, that their children's own sexual orientation was very important to them. Four checked 2, three each checked 3 and 4, one checked 5 (unimportant), and one did not specify. Six mothers decided that they were worried about hereditary influences from the father on their children.

Three of the mothers reported having one child who was gay (daughter 18, son 19, son 23). This represents 11.54% of the 26 children age 16 and older.

Several of the other children indicated their willingness and desire to participate in a study of their own experiences of growing up with a heterosexual mother and a bisexual or homosexual father. One adult daughter is active in setting up a support group for other children who are going through experiences similar to the ones she had to deal with.

Characteristics of Marriages Wives Thought Would Last

Only three wives felt quite sure that their marriages would last. One of these three marriages is now breaking up at the husband's request. Only long-term follow-up studies will provide valid data about conditions under which such heterogeneous marriages might survive and perhaps flourish.

The three women who felt confident in the longevity of their marriages had several things in common. All of them have husbands who consider themselves bisexual. All are highly educated and financially independent, or capable of being so. Their husbands are caring and communicate well with their wives. One wife knew about her husband's bisexuality before marriage, one had been told about her husband's adolescent homosexuality and that it was thought to be cured. The third wife was told after 1 1/2 years of marriage that her husband was experimenting with homosexual sex. Her husband joined her in marital counseling. All three women had had sexual relationships with heterosexual men before marriage and also had had premarital sexual relations with their husbands. All had open marriage contracts and two have extramarital affairs. The third wife had not yet felt any sexual attraction outside the marriage and reports having "great sex" three to four times per week with her husband. All three consider their religious involvement as casual at most. They all have good support systems, including women or couples in similar marriages.

CONCLUSIONS

Because of the shame of having been blind to the facts, and because of the social stigma of bisexuality and homosexuality and the common belief that homosexual men do not marry, many women have difficulty getting validation for their perceptions and obtaining emotional support for themselves and their family. This study contributes toward greater social awareness and openness to heterosexual women's experiences in marriages with bisexual or homosexual men. A profile of the 21 spouses of homosexual or bisexual men in this study does not reveal any consistent psychosocial characteristics. There is no evidence of pervasive premarital sexual inexperience or difficulty. The majority of subjects were firstborn, supporting Wolf's findings (1982). The many childhood traumas reported by subjects warrant a comparison study with other populations of wives. Most women did not select their husbands for qualities different from those of heterosexual men, they experienced satisfying courtships, and the early periods of their marriage were generally satisfactory. The study did not yield a list of early warning signs to help women predict later homosexual activity in their husbands.

The discovery of their husband's homosexual activity was stressful for all subjects, resulting in feelings of anger, shame, fear, and guilt, and in physical stress symptoms. The reaction was worse if the wife felt uncertain about the future of her marriage. The knowledge of her husband's sexual activity was less traumatic than the knowledge of his emotional attachment to other men because the latter was seen as a greater threat to the continuity of the marriage.

Most of the data were collected before the danger of AIDS was well known. While there were some worries about other sexually transmitted infestations and diseases, only three subjects mentioned AIDS. The effects of the increasing incidence of AIDS on heterogeneous marriages needs to be explored.

In marriages where wives experienced their husbands as deliberately deceitful, the resulting loss of trust was particularly stressful to the relationship. There is a need for the development of conceptual models that help children to integrate culturally influenced deceitful and abandoning behaviors of their fathers toward their mothers in a way that facilitates their own future happiness in marriage.

Slightly less than half of the marriages were intact when the questionnaires were answered, and most of the wives were not sure that their marriages would continue. Only three subjects had complete confidence in the long-term stability of their marriage; one of these three marriages has been dissolved recently by the husband. Characteristics of marriages perceived by wives as durable are open communications, the husband's self-identification as bisexual, and opportunities for the wife to have extramarital sexual relationships together with an ongoing sexual relationship within the marriage. The effects of such bilaterally open marriages on small children need to be explored.

More research is needed to identify if there are common characteristics in women who unknowingly become involved in such marriages. Long-term studies are needed to determine the long-term effects and outcomes for both wives and children as well as their needs for support and counseling. Women considering marriage to a bisexual man need explanatory and predictive frameworks to make choices in the best interest for their own future and that of their children.

REFERENCES

Bell, A. P., & Weinberg, M. S. (1978). *Homosexualities: A study of diversity among men and women.* New York: Simon & Schuster.

Bozett, F. (1982). Heterogeneous couples in heterosexual marriages: Gay men and straight women. *Journal of Marital and Family Therapy, 8,* 81-89.

Bozett, F. (1988). Social control of identity by children of gay fathers. *Western Journal of Nursing Research, 10,* 550-565.

Gay Fathers of Toronto (1981). *Gay fathers, some of their stories, experiences and advice.* Toronto: Author.

Gardener, R. (1977). *The parents book about divorce.* Garden City, NY: Doubleday.

Gochros, J. (1982). *When husbands come out of the closet: A study of consequences for their wives.* Unpublished doctoral dissertation, University of Denver.

Gochros, J. (1985). Wives' reactions to learning that their husbands are bisexual. In F. Klein & T. Wolf (Eds.), *Bisexualities: Theory and research* (pp. 101-113). New York: Haworth Press.

Hatterer, L. (1970). *Changing homosexuality in the male.* New York: McGraw-Hill.

Hatterer, M. (1974). The problems of women married to homosexual men. *American Journal of Psychiatry, 131,* 275-278.

Humphreys, L., & Miller, B. (1980). Identities in the emerging gay culture. In J. Marmor (Ed.), *Homosexual behavior* (pp. 142-156). New York: Basic Books.

Karlen, A. (1980). Homosexuality in history. In J. Marmor (Ed.), *Homosexual behavior* (pp. 75-99). New York: Basic Books.

Kinsey, A. C., Pomeroy, W. B., Martin, C. E., & Gebhard, P. E. (1948). *Sexual behavior in the human male.* Philadelphia: W. B. Saunders.

Malone, J. (1980). *Straight women/gay men: A special relationship.* New York: Dial Press.

Miller, B. (1986). Identity resocialization in moral careers of gay husbands and fathers. In A. Davis (Ed.), *Papers in honor of Gordon Hirabayashi* (pp. 224-246). Edmonton, Alberta: University of Alberta Press.

Nahas, R., & Turley, M. (1979). *The new couple, women and gay men.* New York: Seaview Books.

Sanders, D. (1980). A psychotherapeutic approach to homosexuality. In J. Marmor (Ed.), *Homosexual behavior* (pp. 342-356). New York: Basic Books.

Tripp, C. A. (1976). *The homosexual matrix.* New York: New American Library.

Voeller, B. (1980). Society and the gay movement. In J. Marmor (Ed.), *Homosexual behavior* (pp. 232-248). New York: Basic Books.

West, D. J. (1977). *Homosexuality reexamined.* Minneapolis: University of Minnesota Press.

Wolf, T. J. (1982). *Selected social and psychological aspects of male homosexual behavior in marriage.* Unpublished doctoral dissertation, United States International University, San Diego.

Lesbian Mothers
and the Motherhood Hierarchy

Elena Marie DiLapi, ACSW

University of Pennsylvania

SUMMARY. Societal values determine the appropriateness of motherhood. These values are reflected by a society that believes the married heterosexual woman to be the most appropriate to parent. It is these appropriate mothers who form the apex of a three-tiered hierarchy that consists of women who are defined as (a) most appropriate, (b) marginally appropriate, or (c) least appropriate. This paper explores lesbian motherhood within the social context of American society. The "motherhood hierarchy" is presented as a conceptual framework for viewing lesbian mothers, and evidence from the literature supporting the existence of this hierarchy is integrated throughout the discussion. Special attention is paid to the inappropriate mother, and focus is placed on the antilesbian mythology that supports it.

Societal values determine the appropriateness of motherhood. These values are reflected by a society that has deemed the married heterosexual woman as being the most appropriate to parent. It is

Elena Marie DiLapi, ACSW, is a sexuality consultant and specialist in professional training. She has an MSW from the University of Pennsylvania School of Social Work, where she is currently a member of the adjunct faculty.

This paper was originally presented in 1986 at the Challenge of Parenting in the 1980s, the Second Annual Parenting Symposium.

The author wishes to acknowledge the contributions of Dr. Fred Bozett, Dr. Ronald Filler, Dr. Michelle Fine, Dr. Richard Friend, Ms. Mary Ellen Hartigan, Ms. Patricia Johnson, Ms. Martha Pan, Ms. Elise Karen Segal, and the reviewers for helping to shape this paper. A special note of appreciation to the staff of the Elizabeth Blackwell Health Center for Women, Philadelphia, PA.

Correspondence and reprint requests may be addressed to Elena M. DiLapi, ACSW, c/o Penn Women's Center, University of Pennsylvania, 119 Houston Hall, 3417 Spruce Street, Philadelphia, PA 19104-6306.

101

these appropriate mothers who form the apex of a three-tiered hierarchy that consists of women who are defined as being (a) most appropriate, (b) marginally appropriate, or (c) least appropriate to bear and raise children. The marginally appropriate women might be considered to be those women who fall into the categories of single mothers, teen mothers, disabled mothers, and foster mothers. Least appropriate mothers consist of women who fall into the category of lesbian mothers.

This paper explores lesbian motherhood within the current social context of the American society. The changing family structure provides the historic setting in which women's mothering roles and reproductive rights can be explored. Homophobia and heterosexism are the institutional reflections of social values that create and maintain a social order, and that operate to pose lesbian motherhood as an inherent contradiction.

The motherhood hierarchy is presented as a conceptual framework that reflects the social values that create barriers to lesbian motherhood. Evidence from the literature supports the existence of such a hierarchy and is integrated throughout this paper. Three levels of the hierarchy are explored: (a) the appropriate mother, (b) the marginal mother, and (c) the inappropriate mother. Special attention is given to the lowest level and to the antilesbian mythology that supports it.

This conceptual framework is useful in broadening the understanding of institutional oppression as it affects women's reproductive rights. Greater insight into the social values that oppress women, both lesbian and heterosexual, will equip women to overcome these barriers. Additionally, this conceptualization should inform the ongoing development of legal, medical, and social service practices to stop the perpetuation of the motherhood hierarchy. In this way, it is hoped that full and equal access to motherhood options can be available for all women.

SOCIAL CONTEXT OF LESBIAN MOTHERHOOD

The examination of lesbian motherhood requires a look at demographic trends and an acknowledgment of other factors that create the social context within which women currently exist in the United

States. The changing structure of the American family frames this discussion. Compulsory motherhood (Gordon, 1976) and compulsory heterosexuality (Rich, 1980) are dynamics comprising the basis of this social context. We must recognize both the oppression and power that motherhood brings to women. Likewise, we must examine lesbian motherhood as integral to a broad range of reproductive freedoms for all women.

Changing American Family

The American family is changing. Over the last quarter of a century, the traditional nuclear family structure, which consisted of a male head of household, female homemaker, and their children, has changed. Demographic trends in the areas of divorce, single parenthood, and working mothers have influenced this change in family structure.

As the divorce rate increases and as women continue to join the paid work force, a similar increase in single-parent households is also apparent. From 1960 to 1970 the divorce rate doubled; in 1976 it was predicted that one-third of all married couples in the next 30 years would divorce (Hutter, 1980). In Farber, Primavera, and Flener (1983) close to one out of three children, by 1990, could expect to experience their parents' divorce before reaching the age of 18.

Further, the traditional two-parent family existed in only 36% of the American households in 1980 (Kamerman & Hayes, 1982). Figures from recent census reports show that more than 11.7 million children under age 18 in the United States live with only one parent (Stinnet, Chesser, & DeFrain, 1982). In 1970, one out of every 10 children lived with only one parent; in 1980 it was one out of five and 92% of these lived with their mother. Since 1970, there has been a 43% increase in the number of "families" with no man present (U.S. Bureau of Census, 1980). This increase in female headed households over the past 25 years coincided with the increased visibility of those families headed by lesbian mothers.

In 1982 it was estimated that there were over two million lesbian mothers in the United States (Hanscombe & Forster, 1981). An estimated 10% of women in the United States are lesbians. Of these women, 15% to 20% are estimated to be mothers, and approximately 1.5 million children today live in families with lesbian mothers (McGuire & Alexander, 1985). Thus, significant numbers of American women and children are living within this "alternative" family arrangement.

Women's Role As Mother: Compulsory Motherhood

Traditionally, women's value in society (as prescribed by sex role stereotypes) has been defined and controlled by women's unique ability to reproduce and bear children. Of course, this "Compulsory Motherhood" (Gordon, 1976) is to occur within the socially accepted context of heterosexual relationships with husbands in nuclear family arrangements. Responsible for the raising of their children in the home, women play a critical and essential role in the development and maintenance of the family unit. This role for women has been acknowledged by many feminist writers, among them Barrie Thorne (1982), who stated:

> . . . the family assumes, in addition, a particular sexual division of labor: a bread winner husband, freed for and identified with activities in a separate economic sphere, and a full-time wife and mother, defined in Renate Bridenthal's words as being the core of the family, rather than simply being one member of it. (p. 4)

Paradoxically, these social expectations have limited women's options in life (Ruzek, 1978; Steinem, 1978). This sentiment is echoed further in the work of Nancy Chodorow (1974) ". . . women's motherhood and mothering role seem to be the most important features in accounting for the universal secondary status of women" (p. 45). In reviewing the history of the Women's Health Movement, Sheryl Ruzek (1978) stated, "The social interpretation of sex differences is crucial to attack, for traditionally, biological differences have been used to denigrate women and justify their subjugation and oppression" (p. 28). Thus, the contradictions of compulsory motherhood significantly affect women's reproductive choices and the quality of their lives.

Women's reproductive rights can be viewed within the broader context of reproductive freedom in which all people have access to "good public child care centers and schools, decent housing, adequate welfare, and wages high enough to support a family" (Committee for Abortion Rights and Against Sterilization Abuse [CARASA], 1979, p. 11).

Even as women's roles outside the home have expanded, as evidenced by the increase of women in the work force, these new roles have not replaced the old ones. Rather, new roles for women are seen as additions to the primary role as mother.

Additionally, the unstated assumption of heterosexuality within motherhood ought to be explored within this notion of compulsory motherhood. Women's role as mother is often viewed without acknowledgment of different sexual orientations. Compulsory motherhood continues to exist interacting with heterosexist and homophobic attitudes promoting the notion of compulsory heterosexuality (Rich, 1980).

Homophobia, Heterosexism, and Compulsory Heterosexuality

This paper is based on two salient premises: (a) women's reproductive right to live as lesbians, and (b) lesbians' right to be mothers. Therefore, certain aspects of lesbian oppression must be considered. Homophobia and heterosexism are two significant dynamics affecting lesbian women's right to motherhood.

"Homophobia is the extreme rage and fear reaction to homosexuals. Homophobia is a severe disturbance, one which has a powerful effect on the person who has it as well as on the people with whom he or she comes into contact" (Freedman, 1976). Although homophobia as defined here relates to individual attitudes and behaviors, it embodies an institutional component. A quick review of current and past laws indicate the extent to which homophobia has been institutionalized:

> In most U.S. jurisdictions, discrimination against homosexuals in housing, employment, child custody, and other areas of life is legal; while homosexual behavior is illegal. Gay persons are not covered under any of the national civil rights acts, and most court decisions have held that they are not covered

under the equal protection clause of the U.S. Constitution. These legal restrictions reflect generally held social attitudes. (Weitz, 1984, p. 454)

The recent Supreme Court ruling in *Bowers v. Hardwick* (1986) denying gay men and lesbians protection under the Constitution is a clear example of institutionalized homophobia. In the case of lesbian motherhood, institutional homophobia denies lesbians access to their reproductive rights, including freedom of sexual expression, information on health care, and parenting options. Institutional oppression permeates all facets of society. For example, the women's health movement initially excluded lesbians and lesbian motherhood as essential components of reproductive rights (Hornstein, 1973, p. 3). Homophobia leads to discrimination and is reflected in the literature addressing issues of lesbian motherhood.

Hand in hand with irrational fear and hatred of homosexuals and one's own same sex feelings is the heterosexism reflected in the belief that everyone is or should be heterosexual (Fine, personal communication, 1986). Heterosexism is the assumption of the superiority and exclusiveness of heterosexual relationships and is one of the cornerstones of male supremacy and sexism (O'Donnell, Pollock, Leoffler & Saunders, 1979). "Thus the most pervasive and insidious thing that keeps heterosexual domination going is the control over granting or denying women heterosexual privileges; social and family acceptance, economic security, male legitimacy, legal and physical protection" (CARASA, 1981). Heterosexism has severe consequences for lesbian mothers and, like homophobia, is reflected in legislative efforts to control behavior and deny access to services. The Family Protection Act (1979) is one such attempt and according to Rubin (1984) "is a broad assault on feminism, homosexuals, nontraditional families, and teenage sexual privacy" (p. 274).

In discussing the treatment of lesbian existence within the feminist media, Rich (1980) highlighted the heterosexism found throughout our culture:

In none of [the books] is the question ever raised, whether
. . . women should choose heterosexual coupling and marriage; heterosexuality is presumed as a "sexual preference" of
"most women," either implicitly or explicitly. In none of
these books which concern themselves with mothering, sex
roles, relationships, and societal prescriptions for women is
compulsory heterosexuality ever examined as an institution
powerfully affecting all of these; or of the idea of "preference" or "innate orientation" even indirectly questioned.
(p. 633)

This denial of lesbians and therefore of lesbian (maternal) health
needs creates a situation in which lesbians wanting motherhood are
at an extreme disadvantage when compared to their heterosexual
sisters.

Thus, Rich's article establishing the concept of "Compulsory
Heterosexuality" has great relevance to understanding lesbian
motherhood as it reflects the heterosexism sustained in the hierarchy of motherhood.

The social context of lesbian motherhood is defined by the
changing demographic trends indicating a movement away from
traditional nuclear families toward increased numbers of female
headed households, some of which are headed by lesbians. Lesbian
motherhood highlights the interplay between compulsory motherhood and compulsory heterosexuality as social values defining
women's appropriate role and behavior. It is within this context of
women's role as mother that lesbian motherhood emerges as an
issue for exploration.

EXPLORING THE MOTHERHOOD HIERARCHY

Why a Hierarchy?

Rubin (1984) proposed a hierarchical model for understanding
the interaction of sexual values, sexual practice, and social oppres-

sion similar to the one presented here as the "motherhood hierarchy."

> ... All these hierarchies of sexual values, religious, psychiatric, and popular, function much the same way as do ideological systems of racism, ethnocentrism, and religious chauvinism. They rationalize the well-being of the sexually privileged and the adversity of the sexual rabble. (Rubin, 1984, p. 280)

Gender, sexual orientation, and socially prescribed values form the basis of these socially constructed power relations.

A hierarchy model is useful in describing this system of unequal distribution of power and resources supporting motherhood. Gayle Rubin's (1984) sex gender system acknowledges this inequality: "Like gender, sexuality is political. It is organized into systems of power, which reward and encourage some individuals and activities, while punishing and suppressing others" (p. 309). Likewise, the motherhood hierarchy is organized by differential access to motherhood services and support. In this hierarchy, married heterosexual women are rewarded for being mothers, and lesbians are punished and discouraged by limited resources and options for motherhood.

Components of the Hierarchy

The motherhood hierarchy reflects a range of motherhood options valued differentially as "appropriate motherhood" or "inappropriate (deviant) motherhood." Sexual orientation and family form are the primary criteria for placement on the hierarchy and affect the judgment of who is appropriate for motherhood. Fertility status, method of achieving pregnancy/parenthood, and decisions to parent influence one's placement on the hierarchy.

This motherhood hierarchy operates through formal and informal social policy. Ultimately it determines who has access to reproductive health care and parenthood. Those who fit the "appropriate mother" stereotype have the greatest access to information and resources needed to parent.

For the purposes of this discussion, the hierarchy is divided into three levels: (a) the appropriate mother at the apex, (b) the marginal mother in the middle, and (c) the inappropriate mother at the bottom (see Figure 1).

Given the variety of family structures cross-culturally, any one racial/ethnic group may vary as to the specific description of "appropriateness" for motherhood. Nonetheless, a modified version of the hierarchy is sure to emerge. Every culture has its norms created to maintain the status quo. Likewise, every culture has members who challenge those norms and who question the basic social arrangements of a society. Lesbians of all cultural and class groups will choose to parent. "Lesbians considering parenthood face disapproval of those who do not accept alternative, nontraditional, or

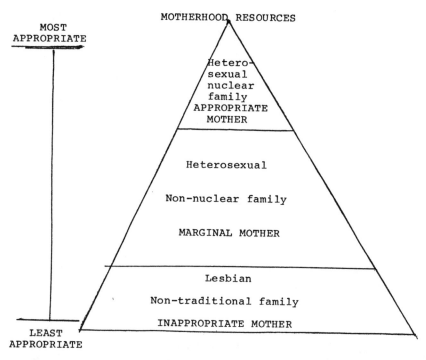

MOTHERHOOD RESOURCES

MOST APPROPRIATE

Hetero-sexual nuclear family
APPROPRIATE MOTHER

Heterosexual

Non-nuclear family

MARGINAL MOTHER

Lesbian

Non-traditional family

INAPPROPRIATE MOTHER

LEAST APPROPRIATE

FIGURE 1. The Motherhood Hierarchy. The motherhood hierarchy is constructed by the social values attributed to various sexual orientations and family forms deeming the appropriateness of certain women for motherhood. Those women forming the apex of this hierarchy have greatest access to motherhood resources, as compared to those valued as less appropriate mothers.

different family styles" (Pies, 1985, p. 19). Within this context, the motherhood hierarchy ought to be further explored for its cross-cultural applicability.

The Appropriate Mother

The appropriate mother stereotype is at the top of the hierarchy. She is a heterosexual woman, of legal age, married in a traditional nuclear family, fertile, pregnant by intercourse with her husband, and wants to bear children. She is likely to be able-bodied, of normal mental functioning, of middle- to upper-middle-class status, and supported primarily by her husband. She may use birth control, which may be dependent on her religion. If she is white, she will probably have access to the health care of her choosing. If she is not white, her health care options will probably be limited. This mother, even though exceedingly rare, still forms the nostalgic image of the "ideal woman" and "ideal mother."

This upper echelon of appropriate motherhood parallels traditional family forms. The standard nuclear family is "composed of husband, wife, and offspring acquired through procreation or adoption, living together in a commonly shared household apart from either set of parents" (Sussman, 1977, pp. 358-359).

> In short, the modern nuclear family, with a particular sexual division of labor, has been writ large as the family and elevated as the only desirable and legitimate family form. A number of critics have set out to demystify the ideology of the monolithic family; but it is feminists who have emphasized the close connection between that ideology and the oppression of women. (Thorne, 1982, p. 4)

The appropriate mother stereotype includes all those women in heterosexual marriages who want to have biological children. Nature, however, does not always produce perfectly fertile partners. In fact, gradations within this upper section are reflected by infertility status of one or both partners and the subsequent options available for having a family.

It is important to remember that these "options" are available almost exclusively to heterosexual married couples (Pies, 1985).

Mainstream institutions such as social service agencies, medical facilities, and legal systems control who has access to these alternative forms of parenthood. In this way, the illusion of the "traditional nuclear family" remains intact working to maintain the "status quo." For example, adoption, insemination, and surrogate motherhood allow families to be created in the absence of conception through intercourse between husband and wife. This "preferred" method of conception reflects the heterosexism previously identified, "the only adult sexual behavior that is legal in every state is the placement of the penis in the vagina in wedlock" (Rubin, 1984, p. 291). Step-parenthood and blended families are options to those who divorce and remarry, or those who marry a partner with an existing family. Fertility status and family structure are variables in this category that may move a woman up or down the hierarchy of appropriate motherhood.

The Marginal Mother

The marginal mother is in the hierarchy's midsection. She embodies various possibilities of child bearing outside the traditional nuclear family.

Located here are those heterosexual women who choose to have children out of wedlock and keep the child (no husband), women who are birth mothers and surrender their child for adoption or foster care, women who are surrogate mothers, or women who choose no children at all. Here again compulsory motherhood reflects the value that places this latter choice in the marginal category at best.

Because family form and sexual orientation are primary considerations for placement on the hierarchy, women who find themselves in this midsection differ from the appropriate mother in terms of family form, and differ from the inappropriate mother in sexual orientation.

These women fail to fulfill their social roles in an appropriate and timely way within the traditional family. Relationship status and decision to parent are critical factors for women in this middle group. "Loss of custody has long been one positive measure used against mothers who engaged in nonmarital sexual behavior . . . there is some recent indication that women are penalized for behavior that a judge is willing to overlook in men" (Polikoff, 1982, p. 191).

Also included here are women who are disabled mothers, foster mothers, teen mothers, single mothers, and working mothers. Nancy Polikoff (1982) highlighted these latter two cases of secondary status motherhood while reviewing court decisions regarding child custody cases. "The mother's employment, even if a matter of absolute financial necessity, is the easiest excuse a judge has to find her the less adequate parent" (p. 159). Additionally, according to social psychologist Dr. Michelle Fine:

> Motherhood as an institution assumes that mother's needs and child's needs are one and the same. For example, if a mother is disabled, it is assumed erroneously that she will have her own special needs and her child's needs would go unmet. Likewise, a mother working outside the home has external demands, the fear is that she will not be able to perform her parenting responsibilities. (Fine, personal communication, 1986)

Polikoff (1982) supported this notion:

> If continuity of primary caretaking is not equated with the best interests of the child, then the judge can make decisions based on the currently popular notion that female headed households create problem children and that the father is a more appropriate authority figure in a patriarchal world. (p. 189)

This marginal status is a consequence of childbearing outside the context of birth/legal children within a heterosexual marriage. Dr. Fine (personal communication, 1986) stated further that an additional underlying assumption regarding motherhood, is that mothers are not or should not be sexual. She pointed to single heterosexual mothers and lesbian mothers as two categories in which a woman's sexuality is presumed to conflict with prevailing social expectations regarding motherhood.

The Inappropriate Mother

The inappropriate mother stereotype is one of deviance. At the bottom of the hierarchy, she has less access to reproductive rights and maternal health services. Here can be found lesbian mothers.

Because lesbian families are seen outside the traditional family form, family structure is often ignored. This is evident in the review of the literature when lesbian mothers are compared to single heterosexual mothers. This occurs despite the literature that suggests that lesbian mothers often receive more support from their cohabiting partners in child care and household duties (McQuire & Alexander, 1985).

Sexual orientation organizes this third and bottom tier of motherhood. This positioning of lesbian mothers is supported not only by compulsory heterosexuality but also the history of child custody cases:

> Lesbian mothers have been and continue to be especially vulnerable to loss of custody as they are perceived to embody both an extreme of unacceptable sexual behavior and an independence from men that removes them from the traditional female role. (Polikoff, 1982, p. 191)

Further, Rubin's (1975) sex/gender system suggests that stigmatized erotic populations are regulated by the social forces around them:

> Individuals whose behavior stands high in this hierarchy are rewarded. . . . As sexual behaviors or occupations fall lower on the scale, the individuals who practice them are subjected to a presumption of mental illness, disreputability, criminality, restricted social and physical mobility, loss of institutional support and economic sanctions. (Rubin, 1984, p. 279)

Weitz (1984) concurred indicating that ". . . stigmatizing as deviant the individuals who challenge traditional ideas may reduce the threat of social change, if these individuals either lose credibility or are removed from the community altogether" (p. 461). Thus, the motherhood hierarchy reflects this attempt to eliminate women who seem to threaten the social order.

The notion of inappropriate mother is supported by the lack of accessibility to adoption, foster care, and insemination services for openly lesbian women. In fact, knowledge of one's sexual orientation may in and of itself preclude some motherhood options. "Lesbians, however, are also confronted with the institutionalized homophobia of these agencies which does not recognize us as credible or desirable parent material" (Pies, 1985, p. 17).

The low status position of lesbians within the motherhood hierarchy is maintained in part by the perpetuation of certain homophobic myths regarding lesbian motherhood. A review of the literature reveals five common myths used against women during custody hearings and more recently in denying access to insemination and other means of achieving motherhood.

Fear of Lesbians Raising Children Without a Father Figure or Male Role Model

Nancy Polikoff (1982) cited the work of Adele Henderickson and Joanne Schulman as exposing the homophobia inherent in this myth, "[They] point out, courts do not value the child's need for male influence enough to require a father to visit his children. If public policy were truly concerned with a continued male presence, it would penalize fathers who failed to exercise visitation rights" (p. 200).

A review of the literature suggests no clear correlation between the absence of the father at home and the acquisition of inappropriate sex role behaviors (Strong & Schinfeld, 1984; McGuire & Alexander, 1985). It is generally understood among professionals in the sex education field that children learn sex roles from many sources—school, church, adults at home, community, television, media, magazines, and movies—and that men and male role models exist for children growing up in lesbian households. Indeed, children in divorced lesbian households spend more time with fathers than those in divorced heterosexual households (Golombok, Spencer, & Rutter, 1983).

Children Growing Up with Lesbians Will Be Gay

This homophobic myth supports the existence of a motherhood hierarchy much like the argument posed by Rubin (1984) of the sexual hierarchy:

> According to this system, sexuality that is "good," "normal," and "natural" should ideally be heterosexual, marital, monogamous, reproductive, and noncommercial. . . . Any sex that violates these rules is "bad," "abnormal," or "unnatural." Bad sex may be homosexual, unmarried, promiscuous, nonprocreative, or commercial. (pp. 280-281)

Research indicates that children of lesbians do not have conflicts or confusion with their sexual identity development. "These studies of children in lesbian households do not support the fear that children of lesbian mothers will be confused about their gender identity, their gender role behavior, and their sexual preference" (McGuire & Alexander, 1985, pp. 183-184). Evidence shows that the majority of lesbians had heterosexual parents and that children of lesbians are overwhelmingly heterosexual, like the general population (McGuire & Alexander, 1985; Hitchens & Price, 1978). When discussing children of homosexual and transsexual parents, Green (1978) highlighted that "all have developed a typical sexual identity, including heterosexual orientation" (p. 696).

Matched studies of children from lesbian single mothers and heterosexual single mothers reveal children of lesbians as developing appropriate gender identity and gender role behavior (Green, 1978; Hoeffer, 1981; Kirkpatrick, Smith, & Roy, 1981; McGuire & Alexander, 1985).

Lesbian Mothers Will Not Provide Adequate Time for Adult-Child Interaction

Throughout the literature there exists an assumption that lesbian mothers, because they are viewed as "single/working" mothers, will not have adequate time to spend with the children and therefore cannot provide well for the child's needs.

This notion is further reinforced by the courts, which "show a strong tendency to judge women's employment more harshly than that of men" (Polikoff, 1982, p. 188). In highlighting this systematic discrimination, Polikoff reported that "the judge noted that the mother's work gave her little time with the children, but there was no reference to a normal working mother's time because normal and 'working' mothers are still considered inconsistent" (p. 189).

This assumption, however, does not hold when one looks at the variety of arrangements that could be made to allow both quality and quantity time with children, despite busy schedules. Strong and Shinfeld (1984), in their review of relevant research addressing this myth, concluded that there is no need to rule out insemination for single lesbian or heterosexual women, based on the unsubstantiated belief that there will not be adequate time for mother to interact with her child (children). Men are not held to this standard, however.

Lesbian Relationships Are Unstable and Do Not Last Long

This myth is rooted in the fundamental heterosexism throughout our culture. By suggesting that lesbian relationships are inconsistent, this myth of relationship instability works to support the "inappropriateness" of lesbians as mothers and family members. According to Weitz (1984), "lesbians also threaten the dominant cultural system by presenting or at least appearing to present an alternative to the typical inequality of heterosexual relationships" (p. 456). Further, Weitz (1984) stated "stereotypes of lesbianism reduce the threat to existing social arrangements by defusing the power of lesbianism as a viable alternative lifestyle" (p. 457).

Various studies of lesbian relationships indicate that lesbian relationships are as stable and mature as heterosexual relationships. Given the unstable nature of the nuclear family, it would be erroneous to suggest that lesbian families are any more unstable than the traditional arrangement (Hitchens & Price, 1979; Strong & Shinfeld, 1984). As previously mentioned, it has been reported that lesbian mothers often receive more support from their cohabiting partners in child care and household duties. For instance, the Bell-Weinberg study, *Homosexualities* (1978), found that homosexual men and women are more apt to have more close friends than their heterosexual counterparts. Thus, one might conclude that lesbians have strong stable support networks and relationships that help to provide consistency for children growing up.

Lesbians Are Sexually Perverse and Molest Children

In response to the growing visibility of sexual minorities, this myth serves to perpetuate the motherhood hierarchy by falsely assigning socially unacceptable behavior to lesbians. "When social norms are changing rapidly, labeling, and punishing certain behaviors as deviant emphasizes the new or continued unacceptability of those behaviors" (Weitz, 1984, p. 461).

However, this myth finds no basis in reality. According to a 1980 publication of the Pennsylvania Department of Education:

> There is evidence that the crimes historically attributed to homosexuals, such as child molestation, are not in fact attributed to them . . . Research by the Kinsey Institute finds, to the contrary, that a much larger proportion of heterosexual than homosexual adults are likely to attempt child molestation. (p. 9)

Mirroring the child sexual abuse literature, The National Gay Task Force (NGTF) stated:

> Every authoritative study on arrests for sex crimes including children indicates over 90% of such incidents involve female children and male adults, and that incidents involving adult women with children of either sex are statistically insignificant. (1979, p. 14)

There are many myths reflecting the homophobia and heterosexism of our culture and these falsehoods are easily dispelled after a review of the literature. However, left unchallenged, these antilesbian myths reinforce the regulation of lesbians as "inappropriate mothers," at the bottom of the motherhood hierarchy.

CONCLUSION

Resistance has always been a powerful response to oppression. The growing strength of lesbian resistance to the motherhood hierarchy parallels the expansion of the ways and means of lesbian motherhood. And yet, the hegemony of the "traditional family" norm pervades, even within the "inappropriate mother" category. This is reflected in the greater acceptance of lesbian motherhood as a result of a previous heterosexual relationship, rather than lesbians choosing motherhood within this "nontraditional" lifestyle.

The "motherhood hierarchy," created on the basis of family form and sexual orientation, reflects as it reinforces cultural norms and social values. By exploiting the stigmatization of women generally and lesbians specifically, public policies and institutional practices minimize the threat to the social order by attacking sex education that validates all sexual orientations, and by favoring traditional nuclear family arrangements created by married heterosexual couples. Such activity has been enacted in bills and laws suggesting the sole legality of heterosexual intercourse within marriage, by the courts in child custody hearings, adoption, and foster care placement decisions, and by major public institutions, including the education and health systems. The 1986 Supreme Court decision in the *Bowers v. Hardwick* case denying homosexuals equal protection under the Constitution is a clear example of the institutionalization of antilesbian/gay values. These institutional barriers reinforce the motherhood hierarchy and attempt both to limit the open acknowledgment of lesbianism as an acceptable sexual orientation as well as act as a deterrent to supporting lesbian headed households as a legitimate family form.

Lesbians have in the past and will continue in the future to choose motherhood. In refusing to accept homophobic and heterosexist assumptions, lesbians confront the motherhood hierarchy. This hierarchy supports married heterosexuals as the only "appropriate mother," frowns upon "marginal mothers," and discourages lesbian motherhood by labeling these women as "inappropriate mothers." But as always with women's positions, even positions high on the hierarchy are not lifelong guaranteed. One may drop status from appropriate mother overnight due to a change in family structure (i.e., divorce, widowhood, unemployment of husband) or by claiming a lesbian identity.

The motherhood hierarchy must be continually critiqued and challenged. The interplay between the changing American family structure, women's mothering role, homophobia, and heterosexism create the social context within which the motherhood hierarchy is constructed. The institutionalization of motherhood through compulsory motherhood and compulsory heterosexuality continue to maintain control over women's lives. We must consider the ways in which the motherhood hierarchy shapes the kind, quality, and availability of medical, legal, and social service resources for women, even as new services are developed by and for the women's community. Attention must be paid to the ways in which lesbians are relatively denied access to motherhood, so that these partialities can be corrected. The nature of the barriers to social change must be understood. The existence of the motherhood hierarchy is one way to examine this resistance.

REFERENCES

Bell, A. P. & Weinberg, M. S. (1978). *Homosexualities: A study of diversity among men and women*. New York: Simon & Schuster.

Committee for Abortion Rights and Against Sterilization Abuse. (1979). *Women under attack: Abortion, sterilization abuse and reproductive freedom*. New York: Ros Petchesky working with Rayna Rapp.

Chodorow, N. (1974). Family structure and feminine personality. In M. Z. Rosuldo & L. Layhere (Eds.), *Women, culture, and society* (pp. 43-66). Stanford, CA: Stanford University Press.

Farber, S., Primavera, J., & Flener, R. (1983). Older adolescents and parental divorce: Adjustment problems and mediators of coping. *Journal of Divorce, 72*, 59-73.

Freedman, M. (1976). Homophobia. *Blueboy: The National Magazine about Men*, Vol. 5.

Golombok, S., Spencer, A., & Rutter, M. (1983). Children in lesbian and single parent households: Psychosexual and psychiatric appraisal. *Journal of Child Psychology, 24*, 551-572.

Gordon, L. (1976). *Women's body, women's right: A social history of birth control in the U.S.* New York: Viking/Penquin.

Green, R. (1978). Sexual identity of 37 children raised by homosexual or transexual partners. *American Journal of Psychiatry, 135*, 692-697.

Hanscombe, E., & Forster, J. (1981). *Rocking the cradle: Lesbian mothers, a challenge in family living*. Boston: Alyson Publications.

Hitchens, D., & Price, B. (1978). Trial strategy in lesbian mother custody cases: The use of expert testimony. *Women's law forum*. San Francisco Golden Gate University Law Review.

Hoeffer, B. (1981). Children's acquisition of sex-role behavior in lesbian mother families. *American Journal of Orthopsychiatry, 51*, 536-544.

Hornstein, F. (1973). *Lesbian health care*. Unpublished manuscript.

Hutter, M. (1980). *The changing family: Comparative perspectives*. New York: John C. Wiley & Sons.

Kamerman, S. B., & Hayes, C. D. (Eds.). (1982). Families that work. *Children in a changing world*. Washington, DC: National Academy Press.

Kirkpatrick, M., Smith, C., & Roy, R. (1981). Lesbian mothers and their children: A comparative survey. *American Journal of Orthopsychiatry, 51*, 545-551.

McGuire, M., & Alexander, N. (1985). Artificial insemination of single women. *Fertility and Sterility, 43*, 182-184.

National Gay Task Force (NGTF). (1979). *Twenty questions about homosexuality*. New York: Author.

O'Donnell, M. et al. (1979). *Lesbian health matters: A resource book about lesbian health*. Santa Cruz, CA: Santa Cruz Women's Health Collective.

Pennsylvania Department of Education. (1980). *What is a sexual minority anyway?* Harrisburg, PA: Pennsylvania Department of Education.

Pies, C. (1985). *Considering parenthood: A workbook for lesbians*. San Francisco: Spinsters Ink.

Polikoff, N.D. (1982). Gender and child custody determination: Exploring the myths. *Women's Rights Law Reporter*, pp. 183-202.

Rich, A. (1980). Compulsory heterosexuality and lesbian existence. *Signs: Journal of Women in Culture and Society*. Chicago: University of Chicago Press.

Rubin, G. (1984). Thinking sex: Notes from a radical theory of the politics of sexuality. In C. Vance (Ed.), *Pleasure and danger: Exploring female sexuality* (pp. 267-319). Boston: Routledge & Kegan Paul.

Ruzek, S. B. (1978). *The women's health movement: Feminist alternatives to medical control*. New York: Praeger.

Steinem, G. (1978). The politics of supporting lesbianism. In G. Vida (Ed.), *Our right to love: A lesbian resource book*. Englewood Cliffs, NJ: Prentice-Hall.

Stinnet, N., Chesser, B., & DeFrain, J. (Eds.). (1982). *Building family strength*. Lincoln, NE: University of Nebraska Press.

Strong, C., & Schinfeld, J. S. (1984). The single woman and artificial insemination by donor. *Journal of Reproductive Medicine, 29*, 293-299.

Sussman, M. B. (1977). *Family*. Encyclopedia of Social Work (Vol. 1, pp. 377-368). New York: National Association of Social Workers.

Thorne, B. (1982). Feminist rethinking of the family: An overview. In B. Thorne

& M. Yalon (Eds.), *Rethinking the family: Some feminist questions* (pp. 4-24). New York: Longman.

United States Bureau of Census. (1980). Household and family characteristics. *Current Population Reports.* (Series P20-366).

Weitz, R. (1984). What price independence? Social reactions to lesbians, spinsters, widows, and nuns. In J. Freeman (Ed.), *Women: A feminist perspective* (pp. 454-464). Berkeley, CA: Mayfield.

A Comparative Study of Self-Esteem of Adolescent Children of Divorced Lesbian Mothers and Divorced Heterosexual Mothers

Sharon L. Huggins, RN, MS

Los Angeles, California

SUMMARY. Thirty-six adolescent children, ages 13 to 19 years, divided equally into two groups according to their mother's sexual object choice and within group by sex, were compared to determine if there were any significant differences in the self-esteem of these two populations. Findings of the analysis of the self-esteem scores indicated there was no significant statistical differences in the self-esteem scores between adolescents with divorced lesbian mothers and adolescents with divorced heterosexual mothers.

There has been much controversy over the years regarding a lesbian mother's ability to provide a healthy psychological environment in which her children can grow and develop. This concern is most evident with child disposition issues, whether it be divorce custody, foster home placement, or adoption. As these emotionally charged issues continue to be highly publicized, it is imperative that decisions that affect the lives of children be made on the basis of empirical data rather than assumptions or personal emotions.

The most common concerns raised are that the mother's sexual orientation will influence the child's sexual choices, that the child

Sharon Huggins, RN, MS, is a mental health nurse practitioner in private practice in Los Angeles, California.

Correspondence and requests for reprints may be addressed to her office at 1514 N. Crescent Heights Boulevard, Los Angeles, CA 90046.

will have an unclear or improper gender identity, and that the child will suffer from a social stigma in peer group relationships.

Recent studies have indicated that parental homosexuality does not give rise to gender identity confusion, inappropriate gender role behavior, psychopathology, or homosexual orientation in children. In four separate studies, investigators found that children of lesbian mothers were virtually indistinguishable along any of these dimensions from children of heterosexual single or divorced mothers when such factors as socioeconomic status, age of children, birth order, family constellation, and length of absence of father or adult male were rigorously controlled (Golombok, Spencer, & Rutter, 1983; Hoeffer, 1981; Kirkpatrick, Roy, & Smith, 1981; Mandell & Hotvedt, 1980).

Therefore, the first two concerns are not documented by research. The child of a homosexual parent is no more likely than any other child to become homosexual or to develop gender identity confusion. The third concern is that the child will suffer from a social stigma in peer group relationships. This is the concern chosen for examination in this study.

There have been no previous research studies of children of lesbian mothers that focuses specifically on the adolescent child. The study of the adolescent child is crucial because the adolescent stage of development is when stigmatization is most obvious and object choice and gender identity are easier to confirm.

METHOD

The design of this study was a comparative survey. The tool utilized to determine self-esteem was the Coopersmith Self-Esteem Inventory (SEI). Stanley Coopersmith (1967) has done the most extensive research to date on self-esteem. His original study consisted of 1,748 children attending public schools in central Connecticut. His Self-Esteem Inventory (SEI) consists of a 58-item pencil and paper questionnaire. It is an internal scale tool divided into five sub-scales: General Self (26 items), Social Self-Peers (8 items), Home-Parents (8 items), Lie Scale (8 items), and School-Academic (8 items). Coopersmith provided overall norms for male and female adolescents aged 9 to 15 years and developed the tool specifically to measure self-esteem.

Spatz and Johnston (1973) administered the SEI to over 600 students in grades 5, 8, and 12 in a rural school district. From each grade, 100 inventories were selected and Kuder-Richardson reliability estimates (KR20s) were calculated. Obtained coefficients were .81 for grade 5, .86 for grade 9, and .80 for grade 12. Kimball (1972) administered the SEI to approximately 7,600 public school children in grades 4 through 8. The sample included students of all socioeconomic ranges as well as black and Spanish-surnamed students. KR20s were generated for each grade level, and obtained coefficients ranged from .87 to .92.

A study of SEI construct validity was reported by Kokenes in 1978. Her investigation included over 7,600 school children in grades 4 through 8 and was designed to observe the comparative importance of the home, peers, and school to the global self-esteem of preadolescents and adolescents. Her study "confirmed the construct validity of the subscale proposed by Coopersmith as measuring sources of self-esteem" (Coopersmith, 1967, p. 13).

The scoring is done by obtaining the number of correct scores. Negative items were scored correct if the subjects answered "unlike me." Positive items were scored correct if subjects answered "like me." The School Form includes eight items that constitute the Lie Scale. The Lie Scale is always scored separately. To score the Lie Scale, one point is awarded for each Lie Scale item answered "like me." The total score for the Lie Scale is obtained by summing the points awarded on the eight items. A high Lie Scale score suggests defensiveness in responses. In such instances, the inventory may be invalid, warranting further evaluation.

To arrive at the Total Self Score, the number of self-esteem items answered correctly are summed. For the School Form, the total raw score is multiplied by two. This results in a maximum self score of 100. For the Adult Form, the total raw score is multiplied by four. This also results in a maximum possible Total Self Score of 100. Both the School Form and Adult Form were utilized depending on the age of the adolescent. High scores on the SEI are generally interpreted as corresponding to high self-esteem. By employing position in the group as an index of relative self-appraisal, one can generally consider the upper quartile as indicative of high self-esteem, the lower quartile generally as indicative of low self-esteem, and the interquartile range generally as indicative of medium self-esteem (Coopersmith, 1967). Also included in the study were interviews with the children and their mothers. Interviews were used to obtain demographic data and explore how the children felt about their parents' divorce. The children with lesbian mothers were also asked specific questions regarding their mothers' lesbianism and what effect, if any, it had on their lives.

The subjects and their mothers were drawn from a nonclinical, nonlegal population. The subjects were contacted through their mothers. The referrals were obtained by solicitation and personal referral by the study participants. All the adolescents completed the SEI and both the adolescents and their mothers were interviewed by the author. The subjects of the study included 36 adolescent children, ages 13 to 19 years, from 32 families, and they were divided into two groups of 18 depending on their mothers' sexual object choice. Each group contained nine female and nine male adolescents, which made possible a within group sex comparison. There were four sibling groups of two children each.

All children and their mothers were presently living in southern California, an area of great visibility for the lesbian and gay community. Although there is a generalized tolerance for the homosexual community, discrimination and prejudice against the concept of lesbian and gay parents or parental figures continues.

To be asked to participate in the study, the children had to be aged 13 to 19 years and be living with their self-designated lesbian mother or self-designated heterosexual mother. The children were the biological products of a heterosexual marriage that had ended in divorce at least one year prior to the time of the study. Also, adolescent children with lesbian mothers must have known of their mothers' lesbianism at least one year prior to the study. It was assumed that the extraneous variables of psychological trauma and loss would be the same for both groups of adolescents. The biological mother had to have physical custody of the child for inclusion in the study. All the children, mothers, and fathers in the sample were Caucasian.

RESULTS

A *t* test and analysis of variance were used to test the hypothesis that the self-esteem of adolescents of divorced lesbian mothers was not significantly different than the self-esteem of adolescents of divorced heterosexual mothers. A *t* test for independent means was used to compare the two groups on other factors that could influence the SEI scores; specifically, age of adolescent, number of times they moved before and after the divorce, and the number of different schools they attended before and after the divorce. No significant differences between the children of heterosexual and lesbian mothers were found for the age of the interviewed adolescent, the number of times the family moved prior to the divorce, or the number of schools the children attended prior to the divorce. However, adolescents with divorced lesbian mothers moved more than twice as often after the divorce and attended almost three times as many schools.

Demographic data on the mothers were compared with a *t* test for independent means. The mean ages of the heterosexual and lesbian mothers were 43.3 years and 42.6 years, respectively. The mothers reported being married the first time a mean of 21.2 years for heterosexual mothers and 22.2 years for lesbian mothers. Neither of these differences were significant. The first marriage of heterosexual mothers was 4.2 years longer than lesbian mothers. Heterosexual mothers had 2.4 children, compared to 1.7 for the lesbian mothers. Heterosexual mothers reported being married a mean of 1.4 times, with four of the mothers marrying twice and two of the mothers being married three times.

No lesbian mothers remarried, although 10 of the 16 lesbian mothers were currently living with a lesbian lover. Only 4 of the 16 heterosexual mothers were either remarried or currently living with a heterosexual lover. The mean SEI scores for the adolescents whose heterosexual mothers married once was 76.7, twice was 84.5, and three times was 73.0.

Table 1 shows results of the Coopersmith Self-Esteem Inventory (SEI) as conducted on 36 adolescents, aged 13 to 19 years. Daughters of the heterosexual mothers scored highest with a mean SEI score of 83.3 and a standard deviation of 9.7. Sons of heterosexual

Table 1

Level of Adolescent Self-Esteem Comparison by Sex
of Adolescent and Sexual Identity of Mother

Sex of Adolescent	[a]Heterosexual Mean (SD)	[b]Lesbian Mean (SD)	Row Means (SD)
Male	72.7 (12.1) $n = 9$	78.7 (13.7) $n = 9$	75.7 (13.0) $n = 18$
Female	83.3 (9.7) $n = 9$	73.4 (22.1) $n = 9$	78.4 (17.3) $n = 18$
Mother's Identity	78.0 (12.1) $n = 18$	76.1 (18.1) $n = 18$	

Note. Overall mean = 77.0; SD = 15.1.

[a]Heterosexual = Adolescents of heterosexual mothers.

[b]Lesbian = Adolescents of lesbian mothers.

mothers had the lowest SEI scores with a mean of 72.7 and a standard deviation of 12.1. Sons of lesbian mothers scored 78.7, with a standard deviation of 13.7. Daughters of lesbian mothers scored 73.4, with a standard deviation of 22.1. The mean SEI scores for all adolescents with heterosexual mothers was 78.0, with a standard deviation of 12.1; and the mean SEI score for all adolescents with lesbian mothers was 76.1, with a standard deviation of 18.0. A two-way analysis of variance was done to analyze these SEI scores further. No significant main effects or interaction effects for either sex of the child or sexual identity of the mother were found.

Table 2 shows the comparison of self-esteem scores for adolescents with single mothers and adolescents with mothers currently living with a lover or remarried. As shown in the table, both children of lesbian mothers and heterosexual mothers had higher SEI scores if their mothers were currently living with a lover or were remarried. The mean SEI score for adolescents with lesbian mothers varied from a mean of 71.6 to 78.3, and the adolescents with heterosexual mothers had mean scores ranging from 76.3 to 82.4. This difference in SEI scores was consistent with both male and female adolescents of lesbian and heterosexual mothers. The mean SEI score for all adolescents with single mothers was 74.8, and the mean SEI score for all adolescents whose mothers were living with a lover or remarried was 79.5.

In reviewing the data, one additional finding warranted further analysis. As shown in Table 1, the mean SEI score for daughters of lesbian mothers was 73.4 and the standard deviation was 22.1. In examining these data, I found there were two distinct groups of SEI scores within the daughters of the lesbian mothers. Four daughters had extremely high SEI scores with a mean of 95.8, and five daughters had extremely low SEI scores with a mean of 55.6. The most striking difference was that only one of four of the high self-esteem daughters felt negatively about her mother being lesbian, whereas 4 of 5 of the low self-esteem daughters felt negatively about their mothers' lesbianism. The lesbian mothers with daughters with low self-esteem had been married 4.4 years longer than the lesbian mothers with high self-esteem daughters. Another finding was that 3 of 4 of the mothers with high self-esteem daughters were currently living with lesbian lovers, but only one of four of the lesbian mothers

Table 2

Level of Adolescent Self-Esteem Comparison by Gender

of Adolescent and Current Relationship Status of Lesbian

and Heterosexual Mothers

	Single Mean (SD)		Couple Mean (SD)	
	Male	Female	Male	Female
Homosexual mothers	77.0	69.0	79.1	77.2
	(1.4)	(21.1)	(15.7)	(24.8)
	n = 2	n = 4	n = 7	n = 5
Mean	71.6		78.3	
Heterosexual mothers	67.2	80.0	79.5	94.0
	(12.3)	(9.5)	(9.3)	(0)
	n = 5	n = 8	n = 4	n = 1
Mean	76.3		82.4	
Column mean	74.8		79.5	
SD	(13.8)		(16.7)	
	N = 19		N = 17	

with low self-esteem daughters was currently living with a lesbian lover. Adolescent daughters with high self-esteem had been told of their mothers' lesbianism at a mean age of 6.0 years. In contrast, adolescent daughters with low self-esteem had been told at a mean age of 9.6 years.

Another important finding that appeared to influence self-esteem among the daughters of lesbian mothers related to their relationships with their fathers. In most cases, contact between father and daughter was limited, but the attitude of the father toward the mother's lesbianism appeared to be the critical factor. An analysis of the data relative to the fathers of the four high self-esteem daughters revealed that two were deceased, one was homosexual and had not seen his daughter for 3 years, and one expressed an accepting attitude toward his ex-wife's lesbianism. This was the only adolescent of the 18 lesbian mothers who related that she could talk to her father about her mother's lesbianism. She stated, "Both my mom and my dad said it was OK that my mom was a lesbian so that made it easier." This particular child had extremely high self-esteem, as did her adolescent brother.

In contrast, two of the five low self-esteem daughters had been separated from a sibling in custody disputes focused on the mother's lesbianism. One had had no contact with her father since infancy, and the father of two refused to discuss the issue with either the children or their mother. In the latter case, despite the fact that their mother was openly lesbian, the children maintained an attitude of secrecy toward the lesbian issue. The younger of the two questioned the impact the secret might have on her ability to relate to others.

There were two sibling groups of two in the lesbian mothers' sample and two sibling groups of two in the heterosexual mothers' sample. In all four sibling groups the SEI scores for the siblings were consistent with each other. Either both siblings scored very high or both siblings scored very low. One sibling group in both sample groups scored very high and one sibling group scored very low.

DISCUSSION

The findings of this study indicate there were no significant statistical differences between the SEI scores of adolescent children with divorced heterosexual mothers and adolescent children with divorced lesbian mothers. Daughters of heterosexual mothers had the highest mean SEI scores and sons of heterosexual mothers had the lowest mean SEI scores. The scores of daughters and sons of lesbian mothers fell in the middle. The mean SEI score for all adolescents of lesbian mothers was 76.1, with a standard deviation of 18.0, and the mean SEI score for all adolescents with heterosexual mothers was 78.0, with a standard deviation of 12.1. A two-way analysis of variance was done to analyze these scores further. No significant main effects for either sex of the child or sexual identity of the mother were found.

The results would suggest that the mother's sexual object choice does not appear to influence negatively the self-esteem of her adolescent children. Therefore, the assumption that children of lesbian mothers are socially stigmatized by their mothers' sexual choice is not borne out by this study. The present study puts into question the use of the mother's sexual orientation as a criterion for determining child disposition issues. This outcome is consistent with the literature on self-esteem that states that the development of self-esteem is primarily influenced by the interaction between children and their parents or primary care-givers. An analysis of other results in this research study offers additional insights into the factors that influence self-esteem.

Comparing the two adolescent groups on the basis of age, number of moves before and after the divorce, and number of schools attended before and after the divorce, it was found that adolescents with divorced lesbian mothers moved more than twice as often after the divorce and attended almost three times as many schools after the divorce. This would suggest that while the lesbian mothers and their adolescent children experienced more disruption in their living environments, these changes did not appear to affect adversely the self-esteem of the adolescents.

The two groups of mothers were compared on the basis of age, age at first marriage, duration of first marriage, number of children, and number of times married. The only differences were that six of the heterosexual mothers remarried, whereas none of the lesbian mothers remarried. This finding is consistent with the self-identity of the lesbian mothers.

Children of both lesbian mothers and heterosexual mothers had higher SEI scores if their mothers were currently living with a lover or remarried. This difference in SEI scores was consistent with both male and female adolescents of lesbian and heterosexual mothers.

This would indicate that whether the mother was lesbian or heterosexual, these adolescents felt better about themselves if their mothers were in a stable live-in relationship. These data, therefore, seem to bring into question the validity of denying child custody to a lesbian mother currently living with her female lover.

A finding that surfaced unexpectedly was the wide variance among the SEI scores of the nine daughters of lesbian mothers. While a sample of four high scores and five low scores precludes any definitive conclusions, it does warrant further research. Results indicated that four factors distinguished the high self-esteem daughters from their low self-esteem counterparts.

First, only one of four of the high self-esteem daughters felt negatively about her mother being lesbian, whereas four of five of the low self-esteem daughters felt negatively about their mother's lesbianism. The adolescent with low self-esteem was more likely to have a negative view of her mother's lesbianism, which is consistent with the theory of self-esteem development indicating that high self-esteem relates to a positive identification with the same-sex parent (Coopersmith, 1967; Farmer, 1980; Hue, 1979). Thus, a negative view of the mother would negatively affect the child's own self-esteem.

Second, three of four of the high self-esteem daughters lived in homes in which the mother lived with a lesbian lover. In contrast, only two of five of the low self-esteem daughters did. This is consistent with the findings discussed previously relating self-esteem to the presence or absence of a stable live-in relationship.

The third factor was the father's acceptance or nonacceptance of the mother's lesbianism, which appears to have an important influence on the child's acceptance. It could be speculated that the daughter with high self-esteem who has limited contact with her father finds it easier to have a noncritical view of her mother's lesbianism. If the father has a negative perception of the mother's lesbianism, the children may need to withdraw from the father in order to incorporate a positive identification with the mother. Conversely, if children identify with the father, they may feel a need to reject their mother and her lifestyle. Further research is necessary on this point, such a study focusing perhaps on the father's perception of the mother's lesbianism and the messages the father might communicate to the child about the mother.

The fourth difference between the two groups was the age at which the daughter learned of her mother's lesbianism. The mean age at which the low self-esteem daughters learned of their mothers' lesbianism was 9.6 years. The mean age at which the high self-esteem daughters learned was 6.0 years. The meaning and implications of this finding are unclear, and the small sample size makes any interpretation of these data difficult. Clearly, this is an area in which more research is indicated.

The last finding explored in this research study was a consideration of the four sibling groups. Sibling scores were consistent with each other independent of the child's gender, indicating that the self-esteem within a family unit is consistent and influenced by factors other than gender.

Although the sexual orientation of the children was not specifically investigated, it is interesting to note that only one adolescent of the 36 interviewed was self-designated as homosexual. This adolescent was from the heterosexual mothers' sample. Many of the adolescents discussed sexuality, but no others felt they were homosexual at this point in their lives. Although this is a limited sample, the study would indicate that growing up in a lesbian household is not necessarily the source of homosexual orientation.

Future research on lesbian mothers must compare lesbian couples with heterosexual couples and single lesbian mothers with single heterosexual mothers. Past research has not held this variable constant, therefore producing invalid comparisons. Given the limitations of this study, it is difficult to generalize these findings beyond the study population. Nevertheless, the data suggest that growing up in a lesbian household does not in and of itself have a negative impact on the adolescent's self-esteem and is therefore not a valid criterion upon which to base child disposition decisions.

REFERENCES

Coopersmith, S. (1967). *The antecedents of self-esteem*. San Francisco: W. H. Freeman.

Farmer, S. A. (1981). Maternal correlates of adolescent self-concepts and adolescent self-esteem (Doctoral dissertation, Georgia State University, 1981). *Dissertation Abstracts International, 41*, 2755B.

Golombok, S., Spencer, A., & Rutter, M. (1983). Children in lesbian and single-parent households: Psychosexual and psychiatric appraisal. *Journal of Child Psychology and Psychiatry, 24*, 551-572.

Hoeffer, B. (1981). Children's acquisition of sex-role behavior in lesbian-mother families. *American Journal of Orthopsychiatry, 51*, 536-544.

Hue, P. T. (1979). An investigation of the relationship between adolescents' self-esteem, perceived parent-child communication satisfaction and feelings toward parents (Doctoral dissertation, University of Houston, 1979). *Dissertation Abstracts International, 40*, 1280-1281S.

Kimball, O. M. (1972). Development of norms for the Coopersmith Self-Esteem Inventory: Grades 4 through 8 (Doctoral dissertation, University of Colorado, 1973). *Dissertation Abstracts International, 34*, 1131-1132S.

Kirkpatrick, M., Roy, R., & Smith, C. (1981). Lesbian mothers and their children: A comparative survey. *American Journal of Orthopsychiatry, 51*, 545-551.

Kokenes, B. (1978). A factor analytic study of the Coopersmith Self-Esteem Inventory. *Adolescence, 13*, 149-155.

Mandell, J., & Hotvedt, M. (1980). Lesbians as parents. *Huisarts and Praktijk, 4*, 31-34.

Spatz, K., & Johnston, M. (1973). Internal consistency of Coopersmith Self-Esteem Inventory. *Education and Psychology Measurement, 33*, 875-876.

Gay Fathers:
A Review of the Literature

Frederick W. Bozett, RN, DNS

University of Oklahoma

SUMMARY. This article reviews the research literature on gay fathers, and includes brief historical perspectives and statistical data. The major portion of the article compares studies of gay fathers with other groups such as lesbian mothers and nongay fathers. Because the literature is sparse, and the research has severe limitations such as small sample size, few definitive statements about these men can be made with certainty. Even so, tentative generalizations are proposed. The article concludes with some suggestions for future research.

The study of both homosexuality and fatherhood has increased dramatically in the recent past. As the viability of gay lifestyles has become more widely accepted, many divorced men and women with and without children have entered the gay community rather than the world of the formerly married (Hunt & Hunt, 1977). There has also been a heightened interest in the expressive function of men, with the role of father garnering the most attention (Benson, 1968; Hanson & Bozett, 1985; Lamb, 1981; Lynn, 1974, 1979; Pederson, 1980). The study of gay men who are also fathers is a logical outgrowth of the studies of homosexuality and fatherhood.

Dr. Bozett is a professor in the Graduate Program, College of Nursing, University of Oklahoma, Health Sciences Center, P.O. Box 26901, Oklahoma City, OK 73190.

Correspondence and requests for reprints may be sent to the author at that address.

137

The purpose of this article is to review the research that has been reported on gay fathers. Limitations of the studies will be mentioned, and directions for further research will be provided.

GAY FATHERS: HISTORICAL AND STATISTICAL PERSPECTIVES

Although the term gay father may seem antithetical, it is likely that gay men have married and fathered children since ancient times. Psychoanalytic, pathologically oriented reports of married gay men appeared in the 1950s and 1960s (Allen, 1957; Bieber et al., 1962; Beiber, 1969; Imielinski, 1969). Anecdotal, more accepting reports began to emerge in the 1970s (Brown, 1976; Clark, 1977; Mager, 1975; Shilts, 1975). The first sociological study, and one of major importance, was reported by Miller (1978, 1979b). Since then, several additional studies have added to the knowledge base on gay fathers.

Although accurate statistics on most aspects of homosexuality are impossible to obtain, estimates of the number of gay fathers can be made. It is generally accepted that 10% of the United States population is homosexual (Churchill, 1971; Kingdon, 1979; Kinsey, Pomeroy, & Martin, 1948). Based on a total population of 230 million in 1983 (U.S. Bureau of the Census), that means there are about 23 million gays in the United States. Also, about 20%, or 4.6 million of the gay male population has been married at least once (Bell & Weinberg, 1978; Jay & Young, 1979; Spada, 1979). Furthermore, it is estimated that 25% to 50%, or from 1.1 to 2.3 million gay men, are natural fathers (Bell & Weinberg, 1978; Miller, 1979a). The actual number of gay fathers is likely higher than these figures suggest because they do not take into account gay men who have married more than once, adopted children, or who are unwed. The number of children of gay fathers is unknown, but combined estimates of the children of gay men and lesbians range from 6 million (Schulenburg, 1985) to 14 million (Peterson, 1984).

REVIEW OF RESEARCH

Although the study of fathers/fatherhood/fathering has increased in the recent past, the research literature on gay fathers remains sparse. The purpose of the following section is to synopsize the research to date. It would be ideal if the studies could be synthesized with an emphasis on their common themes or variables. However, because the few studies available are divergent in their purpose, sampling, and methodologies, this is impossible. Thus, a logical grouping of the studies is made according to whether or not comparison groups were employed. This, then, is the organization that will be followed in this review.

Research in Which Gay Fathers Were the Sole Focus of Study: No Comparison Group

Two major studies (Bozett, 1979, 1980, 1981a, 1981b, 1984, 1985, 1986, 1987, 1988; Miller, 1978, 1979a, 1979b, 1983, 1986) and one less major report constitute the research in this category. The research by both Bozett and Miller were qualitative sociological studies. Data were collected by tape recorded interviews lasting from 2 to 5 hours each. Sample size ranged from 18 to 50. Both researchers claimed to have achieved saturation of the categories generated from the interviews, implying that sample sizes were adequate because additional interviews would not have generated new data. According to Glaser and Strauss (1967), interviews that exceed 25 respondents provide only variation on themes that have already been discovered. The method Bozett used was grounded theory (Glazer & Strauss, 1967), which is an inductive, hypothesis seeking strategy that has as its purpose to generate and suggest, but not test, properties and hypotheses about a general phenomenon. Miller used life history depth interviews utilizing phase analysis (Lofland, 1971) within the social construction of reality framework (Berger & Luckmann, 1966). Both researchers were interested in discovering how men who are both gay and husband/father resolve these apparently conflicting and contradictory statuses or identities.

Bozett derived the theory of "Integrative Sanctioning" to explain the career of the gay father. By participating over time in both the father world and the gay world, the gay father progresses from being attached primarily to the heterosexual world to a primary connection with the gay world. This progression is achieved by means of disclosing his gay identity to nongays and his father identity to gays and receiving mostly positive sanctions, which have an integrative effect. Others' approbations of both identities are introjected into the self as positive, which have the effect of certifying and confirming the two identities of gay and father as compatible and acceptable. Bozett's research was process oriented. It described the gay fathers' objective, public career from before and during marriage, achieving fatherhood, through separation and (usually) divorce to the development of a gay lifestyle.

Paralleling the objective, public career path, the more subjective private career of identity redefinition from heterosexuality to homosexuality is emphasized. Included is an exploration of disclosures and sanctions of the gay identity to various categories of nongays such as wife and children. Equally important is the disclosure of the father identity to gays and their sanctioning, and how the effects of nongays' and gays' responses (sanctions) lead the father to achieve integration. Integration is defined as a state in which the gay and father identities are congruent, and are appropriately overtly manifested; both identities are accepted by both the father himself and others in his proximate social world as nondichotomous. Integration is complete, partial, or absent depending upon whether the father accepts his homosexuality, to whom he discloses it, and how central each identity is to him.

Miller organized his data along a four-point continuum to show the typical steps in gay fathers' normal careers: Covert Behavior, Marginal Involvement, Transformed Participation, and Open Endorsement. The continuum is an ideal-type model, an abstraction of the phenomenon created by emphasizing only the key characteristics in the sequential development of gay fathers' status passage.

Respondents at the *Covert Behavior* point on the continuum engage in furtive sex with other men, but tend to think of this action as nothing more than a genital urge. These men have unstable self-concepts, one day thinking they are homosexual and another day thinking they are not. They operate on the periphery of the gay world trying to compartmentalize gay activities from their family life. During marital coitus, they often fantasize about male erotica. They want to view their marriages as "duties" and do not perceive viable alternative lifestyles. Children are another important reason why these men remain married.

Respondents at the *Marginal Involvement* point on the continuum engage in same-sex sexual behavior and their self-identity, but not their public identity, is homosexual. Compared with men earlier on the continuum, Marginally Involved respondents have an expanded repertoire of gay sexual outlets. Because they are known about by some suspecting audiences, these men often resemble, as one man said, "a crazy quilt of contradictions." Playing the role of the eccentric, engaging in word games of mixed messages, provides a smokescreen for their emotional whereabouts from both gays and nongays. These men are ideologically ambivalent about the gay world, sometimes viewing it as exotic and other times discounting it entirely. Similarly, they have ambivalent commitment to their marriages, occasionally entertaining ideas of divorce. They stay married fearing permanent separation from their children, wanting to avoid stigma, perceiving a lack of viable alternative lifestyles, and unwilling to endure the decreased standard of living necessitated by divorce.

Respondents at the *Transformed Participation* point on the continuum engage in homosexual behavior and have self-identities, and to a limited extent, public identities that reflect acceptance of the validity of their behavior. These men have disclosed to their (ex)wives and parents, but not to their children or employers. Their gay involvement is social and emotional as well as sexual. This acculturation into the gay world involves four areas of concern: (a) disadvantages of advanced age or late arrival on the scene, or both, (b) the necessity of learning new gay social definitions and skills, (c) the need to reconcile prior fantasies to the realities of the gay world, and (d) balancing and compartmentalizing their gay and father roles.

Respondents at the *Open Endorsement* point on the continuum not only engage in homosexual behavior and have public and self-identities reflective of the behavior, but also openly champion the gay community. Initially, there is a political and social tendency toward gay separatism, but over time, the respondents integrate their gay and nongay worlds; homosexuality is blended into their everyday lives. Many of these men have custody of their children, who know their father is gay. Their nonwork activities often revolve around their lover, the children, and a network of friends and organizations, rather than gay commercial establishments.

Miller identified several caveats regarding the moral career continuum. For example, the continuum should not be construed as verifying transient states into types. Additionally, movement out of marriage into an openly gay identity is not unilateral. There are many negotiations back and forth, in and out of the closet. "Doing" and "being" gay involve complex processes with numerous gradations resulting in the blurring of lines between continuum points. There is not a finite number of stages, not every gay father becomes publicly gay, and not everyone passes through every step. Consequently, it is more accurate to talk about career paths, or sets of careers, rather than a single path. Additionally, it is important to stress that few respondents move easily or accidentally from step to step in this career sequence. Rather, each level is achieved by a painful searching process, negotiating with both the self and the larger world.

From his data, Miller drew these conclusions:

1. The event most responsible for initiating movement along the continuum and reconstructing gay fathers' perceptions of the gay community is the experience of falling in love with another man.
2. Factors hindering movement along the continuum include an inability to perceive the gay world as a viable alternative, as well as perceived lack of support from other gays, economic difficulty, family pressure, poor health, wives' dependence, homophobia in respondents or community, and religious/moral scruples.
3. Highly compartmentalized lifestyles, gay celibacy, or deceit sometimes repress open marital conflict, but unresolved tension characterizes gay fathers' marriages. In contrast, men who leave their spouses and enter the gay world report gay relationships to be more harmonious than marital relationships.

4. Respondents report gayness to be compatible with fathering and that the salience of fathering increases once having left their marriages.
5. Men who come out perceive less discrimination from family, friends, and coworkers than those who are closeted anticipate. Wives tend to be upset by their husbands' revelations; the respondents are typically surprised by the positive reactions of their children and their parents.
6. Daughters tend to be more accepting than sons, although most children feel their fathers' honesty brings them closer together.
7. There were few reported instances of neighborhood homophobia directed against gay fathers' children, possibly because the children tried to disclose only to people they knew would react favorably.
8. There was no indication that the children of gay fathers are disproportionately homosexual themselves although, of the children who turned out to be gay, there were more lesbian daughters than gay sons.
9. In spite of the increased public stigma, gay fathers achieved a sense of psychological well-being as their stigmatized careers progressed. This is largely due to their becoming integrated within a supportive gay community that helps reduce cognitive dissonance and neutralizes stigma. Well-being is seen in gay fathers being less anxious, depressed, and guilty about their sexuality, in a reduction of stress-related conditions (ulcers, substance abuse, sleeping and eating disorders), in a stabilization of their self-concept, and in increased congruence between their public and self-identities. In sum, the research of Bozett and Miller are complementary and help to explain the evolution of the gay father identity, or what Miller (1978) referred to as adult sexual resocialization.

The third and last research study discussed in this section is by Skeen and Robinson (1984), who described the family backgrounds of gay fathers. They conducted a nationwide study by questionnaire of subjects from the Catholic gay fellowship Dignity. From their total sample of 285 respondents (a 55% response rate), 30 subjects had fathered one or more children. The principal section of the questionnaire measured respondents' perceptions of mothers' and fathers' acceptance of their homosexuality, description of relationships with parents, parents' expectations, and family atmosphere during childhood. The authors reported that the profile of early family backgrounds of the gay fathers in their study was generally positive. Most subjects were reared in intact homes where heterosexual relationships were role modeled, and unusual amounts of marital discord were not common. Maternal and paternal relationships were described more as adequate and positive than inadequate and negative, although relationships with mothers were perceived to be slightly better than with fathers. Most subjects believed their parents perceived them as worthy individuals, although fathers somewhat less so than mothers. The respondents valued stability of family relationships, even though all were divorced from their wives in favor of homosexual relationships. Both their children and lovers were valued and were listed as important to their lives.

Studies of Gay Fathers in Relation to a Comparison Group

Gay Fathers and Lesbian Mothers Compared

Two studies (Turner, Scadden, & Harris, 1985; Wyers, 1984) are in this category (see Table 1).[1] The purpose of these studies was to identify similarities and differences between the marital and parental behaviors of lesbian mothers and gay fathers as spouses and parents. Both studies utilized face to face structured interviews; the Wyers study employed a pretested questionnaire. The number of respondents in the study by Turner et al. was 10 gay fathers and 11 lesbian mothers, and in the Wyers study there were 32 men and 34 women. All respondents in both studies were Caucasian except for 3 black lesbians. Mean ages of fathers was 37 and 40.1, and for mothers was 35 and 35.5. In the Turner et al. study, the average income for fathers was $24,500, for mothers $13,500. In the Wyers report it was $29,962 for fathers and $13,602 for mothers. Also, the men had more education than women.

Wyers (1984) reported that 10 (31.3%) of the men and 25 (73.5%) of the women in his study were unaware of their homosexuality when they married. This is an interesting finding because

TABLE 1. A Comparison of Selected Variables from the Turner, Scadden, and Harris (1985) and Wyers (1984) Studies.

Variable	Study	Gay Fathers	Lesbian Mothers
Number	Turner et al.	10	11
	Wyers	32	34
Mean	T	37	35
Age	W	40.1	35.5
Mean	T	$24,500	$13,500
Income	W	$25,962.50	$13,602.56
Length of	T	4 - 15	1 - 22
Marriage, Years	W	3-22 (mean = 11)	1-17 (mean =8.6)
Total number	T	17 (11-Male)	20 (8-Male)
of children		(6-Female)	(12-Female)
	W	NR*	NR*
Age	T	4 - 14	7 - 22
of children	W	(Mean = 15.1)	(Mean = 14.38)

TABLE 1 (continued)

Variable	Study	Gay Fathers	Lesbian Mothers
Live	T	NR*	NR*
with children	W	3 (1=part-time)	24 (2=part-time)
Live	T	9	4
with lovers	W	15	12
Children			
do not know	T	2	0
parent is G/L	W	3 (3=not sure)	2
Mean age of			
children at			
discovery of parents			
homosexuality	T	NR*	NR*
	W	11.1	8.1

*NR = not reported

most men come out at 18 to 19 years of age (Dank, 1971; Harry & Devall, 1978; Saghir & Robins, 1973), and lesbians do so in their early 20s (Schafer, 1977; Saghir & Robins, 1973). In both studies, the majority of respondents had been married only once; four women and two men had married more than one time. Length of marriage for the fathers was 3 to 22 years, and for mothers from 1 to 22 years. The men tended to rate their marriages as more satisfactory than did the women. The total number of children for fathers in the Turner et al. (1985) study was 17 (11 males, 6 females), ranging in age from 4 to 14. Mean age of children of fathers in the Wyers study was 15.1 (total number, sex, or age of children were not reported). Lesbian mothers in the Turner et al. study had a total of 20 children (8 males, 12 females), ranging in age from 7 to 22 years. Wyers reported the mean age of lesbian mothers' children as 14.38. In the Wyers study, only one child lived with its father, several children lived with both parents, but most lived with their mothers. Also, mothers commonly had custody. Living arrangements of children were not specified in the Turner et al. study, although it was reported that "all except one gay/lesbian parent had custody of, shared custody of, or [had] regular contact with their children" (p. 9). Nine out of 10 and 15 out of 32 gay fathers were living with lovers, whereas 4 of 11 and 12 of 34 lesbian mothers had lovers. More gay fathers than lesbian mothers reported having good relationships with their ex-spouses. Also, Turner et al. reported that the majority of live-in lovers, both gay and lesbian, acted in the stepparent role.

Turner et al. (1985) asked questions regarding children's sex-role development. Half of the fathers and somewhat more than half of the mothers did not encourage sex-typed toys for their children; the others indicated some encouragement. Most of the parents made efforts to provide an opposite sex-role mode, with fathers making more of an effort than mothers. Nearly all of the subjects in the Turner et al. study reported that their children seemed to be developing "normal" sex-role identification, and the parents perceived them to be similar to other children of their age and sex. Sex-role development was not addressed in the Wyers study.

All of the children of lesbian mothers in the Turner et al. (1985) study knew of the mother's sexual orientation, whereas Wyers (1984) reported that one did not know, and one probably knew but it had not been discussed. Two fathers' children in the Turner et al. study did not know about the father's homosexuality, whereas in the Wyers study 11 of the fathers reported that their children did not know, and 6 fathers were uncertain or sure that all of their children did not know. Reasons the fathers gave for not coming out to their children were fear that it would damage the children, fear of rejection, fear that the children would not understand, the thought that it would be too upsetting, or that is was not their business, and fear of peer rejection, as well as other miscellaneous reasons. Most children of lesbian mothers found out directly from the mother herself. The children of gay fathers may have found out from the father, but were more likely than the children of lesbians to have found out from their mother. In some instances, both spouses told the children, children overheard their parents discussing it, or they figured it out for themselves.

Overall, parents reported that their children's initial reaction to knowledge of their homosexuality had been positive or constituted few if any problems. The range of reactions was from positive with no problems, to mild reactions, to anger and confusion. Some parents reported that they were uncertain of the initial impact. Also, more untoward reactions were reported by gay fathers than lesbian mothers. Overall, current impact was rated as positive for children of both gay fathers and lesbian mothers. The average age of children finding out about mothers' homosexuality was 8, and for fathers it was 11.1 (Wyers, 1984). Children who were told at an earlier age were reported to have had fewer difficulties than those who found out when they were older (Turner et al., 1985).

Wyers (1984) reported that 58.8% of the children of lesbian mothers and 21.1% of the children of gay fathers experience relationship problems with other people because of their knowledge of their parents' homosexuality, although most of the problems are not considered to be serious. Wyers also reported that it was significantly more difficult for gay fathers than for lesbian mothers to acknowledge their homosexuality. Both the men and women stated that having children made the coming out process more difficult. Lesbians most feared losing custody, whereas gay fathers' greatest fear was damaging their children. In Wyers' study, all spouses except two of the men's and five of the women's knew. It is also interesting that, in the Wyers study, less than half of the lesbian mothers and gay fathers indicated support by their families after they learned of the respondents' homosexuality. Lesbians tended to turn to friends for support, whereas it was more common for gay fathers to seek professional assistance. Turner et al. (1985) made the following generalizations from their study: (a) Parents' homosexuality seems to create few long-term problems for children, who seem to accept it better than parents anticipate; (b) most subjects report positive relationships with their children; (c) parents' sexual orientation is of little importance in the overall parent/child relationship; and (d) lesbian/gay parents try harder to create stable home

lives and positive relationships with their children than one would
expect from traditional heterosexual parents.

Gay Fathers, Heterosexual Fathers, Lesbian Mothers, Heterosexual Mothers Compared

One study (Harris & Turner, 1985-1986) compared all four
groups. However, the sample size is exceedingly small for mean-
ingful comparisons to be made: 10 gay fathers, 2 heterosexual single fathers, 13 lesbian mothers, and 14 heterosexual single mothers.
Data were obtained from mailed questionnaires. Ages of the gay/
lesbian (G/L) parents ranged from 29 to 53 years (median = 39),
whereas the heterosexual (H) parents ranged from 19 to 47 years
(median = 25). The majority were Caucasian, highly educated,
and were employed mostly in professional positions. The three major religions (Catholic, Protestant, Judaism) were represented, with
30% of the sample claiming no religion. Four persons had never
married. Several subjects had married from two to five times. Median length of marriage was 6 years. Number of children ranged
from one to seven, with their ages ranging from 5 to 31.

The authors reported that few differences were found between the
G/L and H parents, with the major differences reflecting their sex or
residence, not their sexual orientation. Except for the H parents'
tendency to make a greater effort to provide an opposite sex-role
model for their children, no significant differences were found in
the relationship of the G/L and H parents with their children. Differences found between G/L parents were that the gay fathers had
higher incomes and were more likely to live with lovers or male
friends. Also, they felt more satisfaction with their first child, had
fewer disagreements with their partner over discipline, and were
more likely to encourage play with sex-typed toys. However, lesbian mothers were more likely to realize benefits of their homosexuality for their children in the areas of accepting their own sexuality, increasing empathy and tolerance for others, and exposure to
new points of view. Interestingly, no G/L subject reported that a
spouse or child demonstrated a positive response to the discovery
that the parent was gay. This is contrary to Bozett (1980, 1981b),
who found that several spouses and children reacted positively.

Similar to most parents, G/L subjects admitted to having some difficulties in child rearing and getting along with their children. The authors summarized their findings by stating that being gay is compatible with effective parenting, and that the parents' sexual orientation is not the major issue in these parents' relationships with their children.

Gay Fathers and Gay Non-Fathers Compared

Two brief studies compared gay fathers and gay non-fathers, Robinson and Skeen (1982) and Skeen and Robinson (1985). Both derived their sample from the same members of Dignity as previously described. The study by Robinson and Skeen (1982) compared the two groups on sex-role orientation as measured by the Bem Sex Role Inventory (1974). Categorical scoring was applied to the responses, and comparisons were made to ascertain if there were any relationships between masculinity and fatherhood. The findings indicate that there were none. Gay men who father children were no more masculine than gay men who do not father children. A diverse pattern of sex-role orientation was found in which the subjects scored equally often in the androgymous, masculine, feminine, and undifferentiated categories. Interestingly, gay fathers scored more nonandrogynous (masculine, feminine, undifferentiated). Also, fewer fathers scored masculine than in any other category. The researchers concluded that this study supports other research that indicates that sexual behavior and sex-role orientation are unrelated phenomena, and develop out of separate experiences.

The other study by Skeen and Robinson (1985) compared gay and nongay fathers' relationships with their parents. Data from the same sample of respondents from Dignity were used. Included in the questionnaire were questions that dealt with marital status and children, and relationship with each parent. No differences were found between the two groups' perceptions of their early family life and relationships with their fathers and mothers. Both groups were reared in intact homes without much marital discord, and they perceived their family of orientation as pleasant. Both groups did perceive their mothers as more accepting, yet their perceptions of their fathers were also primarily positive. The authors concluded that this study supports other research that questions the Freudian-based concept of a direct causal link between early family relationship patterns and sexual orientation.

Gay Fathers and Heterosexual Fathers Compared

Scallen (1981) assessed the relationship between sexual orientation and fathers child rearing attitudes and behaviors. Self-assessments of both sets of fathers in the performance of the paternal role were also explored. The sample consisted of 20 homosexual, and 20 heterosexual fathers, and a control group of 20 fathers. The fathers were comparable on demographics of age, education, income, and employment. Data were obtained from responses to the Eversoll Father Role Opinionnaire, the Kinsey Scale, the Father/Son/Daughter Practice Report, and a demographic questionnaire. There were no significant differences between the two groups on the paternal problem solving dimensions, on the degree of emphasis placed on recreation, or on the subjects' self-reports pertaining to the encouragement of autonomy. However, the findings suggest that sexual orientation does have a relationship to espoused paternal attitudes. Gay fathers were found to be more endorsing of paternal nurturance, less endorsing of economic providing, and somewhat less traditional in their overall paternal attitudes than were heterosexual fathers. Gay fathers also appeared to have a substantial psychological investment in the paternal role. Moreover, they demonstrated a significantly more positive self-assessment of their performance in the paternal role than did the heterosexual fathers. Lastly, the data indicate that most subjects in all groups appeared to endorse an active, caretaking stance regarding the paternal role, which, according to Scallen, tends to substantiate the trend toward increasing paternal role expectations.

Studies in Which Gay Fathers Were Part of a Larger Study (Not the Focal Concern)

There are three additional studies, one of which consisted of a large sample from the San Francisco Bay Area (Bell & Weinberg, 1978), and two (Jay & Young, 1977; Spada, 1979) that derived data from international samples (mostly from the United States). The

Bell and Weinberg (1978) study employed structured face to face interviews of 979 respondents, whereas the other two studies used mailed questionnaires with samples that ranged from over 1,000 (Spada, 1979) to more than 4,000 (Jay & Young, 1977). These studies provided important evidence toward the understanding of homosexuality, and also helped corroborate findings from previous studies. In addition, they helped verify qualitative data. Some of the major statistical findings from these studies are presented in Table 2, with emphasis on gay men who married and had children. These data are presented without further discussion.[1]

LIMITATIONS OF THE RESEARCH

Most studies of gay fathers are based on nonrandom small sample sizes, with subjects who are Caucasian, middle- to upper-middle-class, well educated with occupations commensurate with their education, who come mostly from urban centers, and who are relatively accepting of their homosexuality. There is severely limited knowledge of gay fathers who vary from these demographics. Moreover, the validity and reliability of the instruments used in the studies reported are not always addressed. Although the qualitative studies of Bozett and Miller are complementary, their replication with samples with different demographics, from more diverse settings are needed in order to develop a substantive theoretical construct in which practitioners and researchers can have confidence.

GENERALIZATIONS

From this review of the literature, and keeping in mind the limitations just discussed, the following tentative generalizations can be proposed:

1. A significant number of gay men are fathers who usually marry only once.
2. Gay fathers describe their family backgrounds as generally positive.
3. There is no difference between gay and nongay fathers' relationship with their parents.

4. Gay men who father children are no more masculine than gay men who do not father children.

5. Reasons for gay fathers' remaining married are (a) lack of a perceived viable alternative, (b) commitment to their children, and (c) knowledge that divorce would lower their standard of living.

6. Some gay fathers may be relatively content in their marriages, but most are not.

7. Gayness and traditional marital relationships are often discordant compared to relationships established when gay fathers move into the gay world.

8. Two factors that govern the style of gay fathers' sexual expression are (a) whether they live with or without their wife, and (b) the father's degree of occupational autonomy.

9. Awareness of one's homosexuality occurs later in gay men who marry than it does for the gay male population in general.

10. Gay fathers appear to proceed through a relatively predictable process from unacceptance of their homosexuality with little knowledge of the gay world, to acceptance with an increased congruence between their public and self-identities.

11. In spite of increased public stigma, gay fathers achieve a sense of psychological well-being as their stigmatized careers progress.

12. Gay fathers have more difficulty acknowledging their homosexuality than do lesbian mothers.

13. Having children at home makes coming out more difficult for gay fathers.

14. Gay fathers have more difficulty disclosing their gay identity to their children than do lesbian mothers. Moreover, the problem may be more pronounced among black men.

15. Most children's reactions to their gay fathers' disclosure is reported by the fathers as "none" or "tolerant and understanding." Nevertheless, more untoward reactions from children are reported by gay fathers than lesbian mothers.

16. Gay fathers, more than lesbian mothers, report that their children have difficulties with peers because of the parent's homosexuality.

17. Children who are told at an earlier age are reported to have fewer difficulties managing the knowledge of their fathers' homosexuality.
18. Being gay is compatible with effective parenting.
19. The father's homosexuality seems to create few long-term problems for their children, who appear to accept it better than fathers anticipate.
20. Gay fathers usually do not have physical custody of their children.
21. Gay fathers who do not have physical custody of their children tend to maintain consistent contact with them.
22. Most gay fathers report positive relationships with their children.
23. The father's sexual orientation is of little importance in the overall father/child relationship.
24. Gay fathers try harder to create stable home lives and positive relationships with their children than one would expect from traditional heterosexual parents.
25. Gay fathers make efforts to provide opposite sex role models for their children.
26. In comparison to heterosexual fathers, it appears that sexual orientation *is* related to espoused paternal attitudes: (a) Gay fathers are more endorsing of paternal nurturance, (b) gay fathers are somewhat less traditional in their overall paternal attitudes, (c) gay fathers have a substantial investment in the paternal role, and (d) gay fathers assess themselves more positively in their performance of the paternal role.

DIRECTIONS FOR FUTURE RESEARCH

Specific recommendations for research studies will not be listed here because the author has recently done so elsewhere (Bozett, 1985, 1987). The suggestions here address several general challenges that must be accepted if substantive progress in this important area of research is to be made.

First, it is imperative that entire gay father family units be studied. These families take a variety of forms, from single custodial to step- or multifamily households. The patterns of interactions of

TABLE 2. A Comparison of Selected Variables from the Bell and Weinberg (1978), Jay and Young (1977), and Spada (1979) Studies.

Studies	Homosexualities (Bell & Weinberg)	The Gay Report (Jay & Young)	The Spada Report (Spada)
Variables			
Subjects	979	5,291	1,038
Sample Source	San Francisco Bay Area	International	International
Methodology	Structured Interview	Mailed Questionnaire	Mailed Questionnaire
Age	25 - 46 Average age: Caucasian : 36.97 Black : 27.20	14 - 78	16 - 77
Number of Male Subjects	686	4,329	1,038
Race	Caucasian: 575 Blacks : 111 686 Men	Caucasian: 91% All others represented	Caucasian: 858 All others represented
Percent of Married: Past or present	Caucasian: 20% Black : 13%	19%	17%
Married more than once	Caucasian: 15% Black : 0%	NR*	NR*

TABLE 2 (continued)

Marital satisfaction	Majority : Moderately happy to very happy.		NR*	Majority : Not happy
Homosexuality involved in reason for divorce	Caucasian Yes : 54% No : 46%	Black 23% 77%	Separated Yes: 78% Divorced Yes : 45%	NR*
Number of children in first marriage	Caucasian N : 116 ------- % -------	Black N : 14 ------ % ------	NR*	NR*
None	50	29		
One	25	50		
Two	15	21		
Three	5	0		
Four or more	5	0		
Number of children (natural, adopted, step) over 12 who know or suspect father is gay	Caucasian N : 46 ------ % ------ None 61 One 24 Two 15 Three or more 0	Black N : 2 ----- % ----- 100 0 0 0	NR*	NR*

TABLE 2 (continued)

How children over	Caucasian	Black	NR*	NR*
12 found out	N : 14	N : 0		
father is gay	------	-----		
	%	%		
	------	-----		
Father told	36	0		
Spouse told	29	0		
Told by others	7	0		
Guessed/ Surmised	29	0		

Children's overall	Caucasian	Black	NR*	NR*
reaction	N : 17	N : 0		
	------	-----		
	%	%		
	------	-----		
No reaction	71	0		
Tolerant/ understanding	29	0		
Negative reaction	0	0		
Worry, fear for my welfare	0	0		
Indifference	0	0		
Some other reaction	0	0		

TABLE 2 (continued)

Effect of	Caucasian	Black	NR*	NR*
children knowing	N = 17	N = 0		
on relationship	------	-----		
	%	%		
	------	-----		
No effect	76	0		
Strengthened				
relationship	12	0		
Weakened				
relationship	6	0		
Destroyed				
relationship	0	0		
Other changes in				
relationship	6	0		

*NR = Not Reported

family members with one another, the family dynamics, the relationship of the family to supra- and infrastructures, and the process and progress of the family life-cycle over time needs investigation to achieve an understanding of gay fathers and their families, and to determine the effect being reared in such a family has on children's development.

The approach to the study of the gay father and the gay father family must derive from a theoretical framework that is sufficiently inclusive to allow for wide variations of gay fathering styles. Sexual orientation per se does not dictate specific fathering behaviors. Moreover, it is not likely that being gay will guarantee nurturing, sensitive, father/child relationships, as the research to date suggests. Future studies must either generate theory, or be based on theory that is sufficiently encompassing to explain and, more important, predict positive and negative gay father family outcomes. Certainly, not all gay fathers, like not all nongay fathers, are suited to the paternal role. Nor is it likely that all gay fathers carry it out successfully.

Only through ongoing study of gay father family units in their multiple forms, and in their extremes from positive to negative, will an assertion that gay fathering is viable, positive, or even desirable become convincing.

CONCLUSION

In sum, there are only a handful of studies on gay fathers. These studies are highly diverse and provide only a glimpse into this substantive area of study. It is a good beginning. However, much theorizing and research yet needs to be carried out for there to be a comprehensive and objective understanding of the phenomenon of gay fathers.

NOTE

1. More data is presented in these research studies than is reported here. The data included in this article is that which the author believes to be most germain to this review.

REFERENCES

Allen, C. (1957, February). When homosexuals marry. *Sexology*, pp. 416-420.
Bell, A. P., & Weinberg, M. S. (1978). *Homosexualities: A study of diversity among men and women*. New York: Simon & Schuster.
Benson, L. (1968). *Fatherhood: A sociological perspective*. New York: Random House.
Bem, S. L. (1974). The measurement of psychological androgyny. *Journal of Consulting and Clinical Psychology, 42*,155-162.
Berger, P., & Luckmann, T. (1966). *The social construction of reality: A treatise in the sociology of knowledge*. New York: Doubleday.
Bieber, I. (1969). The married homosexual male. *Medical Aspects of Human Sexuality, 3*, 76-84.
Bieber, I., Dain, H., Dince, P., Dreillich, M., Grand, H., Gundlach, R., Kre-

mer, M., Rilkin, A., Wilber, C., & Bieber, T. (1962). *Homosexuality: A psycho-analytic study*. New York: Basic Books.

Bozett, F. W. (1979). Gay fathers: The convergence of a dichotomized identity through integrative sanctioning (Doctoral dissertation, University of California, San Francisco). *Dissertation Abstracts International, 40*, 2608B-2609B.

Bozett, F. W. (1980). Gay fathers: How and why they disclose their homosexuality to their children. *Family Relations, 29*, 173-179.

Bozett, F. W. (1981a). Gay fathers: Evolution of the gay-father identity. *American Journal of Orthopsychiatry, 51*, 552-559.

Bozett, F. W. (1981b). Gay fathers: Identity conflict resolution through integrative sanctioning. *Alternative Lifestyles, 4*, 90-107.

Bozett, F. W. (1984). Parenting concerns of gay fathers. *Topics in Clinical Nursing, 6*, 60-71.

Bozett, F. W. (1985). Gay men as fathers. In S. M. H. Hanson & F. W. Bozett (Eds.), *Dimensions of fatherhood* (pp. 327-352). Beverly Hills, CA: Sage Publications.

Bozett, F. W. (1986, April). *Identity management: Social control of identity by children of gay fathers when they know their father is a homosexual*. Paper presented at the Seventh Biennial Eastern Nursing Research Conference, New Haven, CT.

Bozett, F. W. (1987). Gay fathers. In F. W. Bozett (Ed.), *Gay and lesbian parents* (pp. 3-22). New York: Praeger.

Bozett, F. W. (1988). Gay fatherhood. In P. Bronstein & C. P. Cowan (Eds.), *Fatherhood today: Men's changing role in the family* (pp. 214-235). New York: John C. Wiley & Sons.

Brown, H. (1976). Married homosexuals. In H. Brown (Ed.), *Familiar faces, hidden lives* (pp. 108-130). New York: Harcourt Brace Jovanovich.

Churchill, W. (1971). *Homosexual behavior among males: A cross-cultural and cross species investigation*. Englewood Cliffs, NJ: Prentice-Hall.

Clark, D. (1987). *The new loving someone gay*. Berkeley, CA: Celestial Arts.

Dank, B. (1971). Coming out in the gay world. *Psychiatry, 34*, 180-197.

Festinger, L. (1957). *A theory of cognitive dissonance*. Evanston, IL: Row Peterson.

Glaser, B., & Strauss, A. (1967). *The discovery of grounded theory*. Chicago: Aldine.

Hanson, S. M. H., & Bozett, F. W. (1985). *Dimensions of fatherhood*. Beverly Hills, CA: Sage Publications.

Harris, M. B., & Turner, P. H. (1985-1986). Gay and lesbian parents. *Journal of Homosexuality, 12*(2), 101-113.

Harry, J., & Devall, W. (1978). *The social organization of gay males*. New York: Praeger.

Hunt, M., & Hunt, B. (1977). *The divorce experience*. New York: McGraw-Hill.

Imielinski, K. (1969). Homosexuality in males with particular reference to marriage. *Psychotherapy and Psychosomatics, 17*, 126-132.

Jay, K., & Young, A. (1979). *The gay report*. New York: Summit.

Kingdon, M. A. (1979). Lesbians. *The Counseling Psychologist, 8*, 44-45.

Kinsey, A. C., Pomeroy, W. B., & Martin, C. E. (1948). *Sexual behavior in the human male*. Philadelphia: W.B. Saunders.

Lamb, M. E. (Ed.). (1981). *The role of the father in child development*. New York: John C. Wiley & Sons.

Lofland, J. (1971). *Analyzing social settings*. Belmont, CA: Wadsworth.

Lynn, D. (1974). *The father: His role in child development*. Monterey, CA: Brooks/Cole.

Lynn, D. (1979). *Daughters and parents: Past, present, and future*. Monterey, CA: Brooks/Cole.

Mager, D. (1975). Faggot father. In K. Jay & A. Young (Eds.), *After you're out* (pp. 128-134). New York: Gage.

Miller, B. (1978). Adult sexual resocialization: Adjustments toward a stigmatized identity. *Alternative Lifestyles, 1*, 207-234.

Miller, B. (1979a). Gay fathers and their children. *The Family Coordinator, 28*, 544-52.

Miller, B. (1979b). Unpromised paternity: The lifestyles of gay fathers. In M. Levine (Ed.), *Gay men: The sociology of male homosexuality* (pp. 239-252). New York: Harper & Row.

Miller, B. (1983). *Identity conflict and resolution: A social psychological model of gay familymen's adaptations*. Unpublished doctoral dissertation, University of Alberta, Edmonton.

Miller, B. (1986). Identity resocialization in moral careers of gay husbands and fathers. In A. Davis (Ed.), *Papers in honor of Gordon Hirabayashi* (pp. 197-216). Edmonton, Canada: University of Alberta Press.

Pederson, F. A. (Ed.). (1980). *The father-infant relationship*. New York: Praeger.

Peterson, N. (1984, April 30). Coming to terms with gay parents. *USA Today*, p. 30.

Robinson, B., & Skeen, P. (1982). Sex-role orientation of gay fathers versus gay non-fathers. *Perceptual and Motor Skills, 55*, 1055-1059.

Saghir, M., & Robins, E. (1973). *Male and female homosexuality*. Baltimore: Williams & Wilkins.

Scallen, R. M. (1981). An investigation of paternal attitudes and behaviors in homosexual and heterosexual fathers (Doctoral dissertation, California School of Professional Psychology, Los Angeles). *Dissertation Abstracts International, 42*, 3809B.

Schafer, S. (1977). Sociosexual behavior in male and female homosexuals. *Archives of Sexual Behavior, 6*, 355-364.

Schulenburg, J. (1985). *Gay parenting*. New York: Doubleday.

Shilts, R. (1975, October 22). Gay people make babies too. *The Advocate*, p. 25.

Skeen, P., & Robinson, B. (1984). Family backgrounds of gay fathers: A descriptive study. *Psychological Reports, 54*, 99-105.

Skeen, P., & Robinson, B. (1985). Gay fathers' and gay non-fathers' relationship with their parents. *Journal of Sex Research, 21*, 1-6.

Spada, J. (1979). *The Spada report*. New York: New American Library.
Turner, P. H., Scadden, L., & Harris, M. B. (1985, March). *Parenting in gay and lesbian families*. Paper presented at the First Annual Future of Parenting Symposium, Chicago, IL.
U. S. Bureau of the Census (1983). Statistical Abstracts of the United States (104th Ed.). Washington, DC: U. S. Government Printing Office.
Wyers, N. L. (1984). *Lesbian and gay spouses and parents: Homosexuality in the family*. Portland, OR: School of Social Work, Portland State University.

The Value of Children
to Gay and Heterosexual Fathers

Jerry J. Bigner, PhD
R. Brooke Jacobsen, PhD

Colorado State University

SUMMARY. Responses of 33 gay fathers were compared with those of 33 heterosexual fathers on the Value of Children scale, an empirical measure of the reasons for wanting to become a parent. Responses of gay fathers did not differ significantly from heterosexual fathers on the majority of the items of the inventory, but differences were found on two subscales, Tradition-Continuity-Security and Social Status. Item analysis of responses shows that gay fathers may have particularly significant reasons motivating them to become parents.

THE GAY FATHER ENIGMA

The gay father is an emergent figure in the literature on homosexuality, yet knowledge about these individuals is still scant. Most published information is based on interview and case study material rather than on empirically derived data. Previous studies have used small samples and have not contrasted responses of homosexual with heterosexual fathers. Gay fathers have a unique and more complex social-psychological environment than do other homosexual and heterosexual males, relative to identity concerns, acceptance of self, and acceptance by other homosexuals, as well as relative to parenting and custody issues. Additional concerns relate to gay fathers' development of long-term, committed relationships with men

Correspondence and requests for reprints may be addressed to the authors at the Department of Human Development and Family Studies, Colorado State University, Ft. Collins, CO 80523.

163

who accept and are willing to deal with children as a central issue in the relationship.

The term *gay father* may seem paradoxical because the term "father" usually implies heterosexuality. A further complication results from the stereotype of gay men that is contradictory to the idea or the reality of fatherhood. However, researchers estimate that between 20 to 25% of identified gay men are fathers (Bell & Weinberg, 1978; Maddox, 1982; Miller, 1979; Weinberg & Williams, 1974). Thus, this group appears to constitute a minority within a minority. The actual number of gay fathers cannot be accurately estimated because many remain "closeted" for marital or other reasons.

Some researchers have described the man who is both gay and a father as being a victim of divided personal identity (Bozett, 1981b, 1985; Robinson & Skeen, 1982). Such individuals can be described as marginal to the cultural worlds of both heterosexuals and gays. In that each identity (heterosexual and homosexual) is to some extent unacceptable by the other culture, the task is to integrate both identities into the cognitive class, "gay father." Bozett (1981b, 1985) referred to this as *integrative sanctioning*. This involves the man's gradual disclosure of his gay identity to nongays and his father identity to gays, and forming liaisons with persons who accept both identities. It also involves distancing himself from those who are not tolerant. At the same time, identity development as a gay male is enhanced by participation in a gay lifestyle.

THE "LOW STATUS INTEGRATION" HYPOTHESIS

Typically, gay culture is singles-oriented. Participants are seen as having few long-term commitments to partners, few financial obligations, and as placing emphasis on personal freedom and autonomy (Bozett, 1981b). The gay father, in contrast, is someone with emotional and financial responsibilities to others, time restrictions, different living arrangements, obligations to others who are dependent on him, and so on. It is not uncommon for gay fathers to experience discrimination and rejection from other gays who are not fathers because of these restrictions to freedom and devaluation of the place of children in one's life (Bozett, 1981a). Gay fathers may have had experience in long-term, committed heterosexual relationships and attempt to find this same type of relationship with male partners. Such liaisons could present unusual strains due to feelings of jealousy experienced by the nonparent partner, and the knowledge that the gay father may maintain strong ties to his child(ren).

Such gay fathers are semi-integrated into two subcultures, the homosexual father versus the heterosexual parent. They hold two social statuses that are to some degree inconsistent. Using Gibbs and Martin's (1964) terminology, they are characterized by *low status integration*. The Gibbs-Martin interpretation of the low status integration hypothesis suggests that individuals who hold partly inconsistent statuses tend to have unique experiences as well as role conflicts. Their experiences are not shared with persons with "consistent" statuses; for example, heterosexual fathers and gay males who are not parents. This hypothesis suggests that a gay father's parental role behaviors and reasons for being a parent are unique.

MOTIVATIONS FOR FATHERHOOD

Little empirical evidence is available about gay fathers (Bozett, 1981a; Clark, 1979; Harris & Turner, 1985-1986: Miller, 1979; Voeller & Walters, 1978). Speculatively, their motivations toward parenthood may include: (a) not being able to deal with one's homosexual orientation until after a marriage within which one or more children are produced, (b) choosing to become a father despite one's homosexual preference and identity, or (c) desiring parenthood because of dissatisfaction with a less "rooted" gay lifestyle. Researchers report that while some individuals come to acknowledge their homosexual orientation after marriage, others enter into marriage fully aware of their homosexuality. In the latter case, reasons given for marriage include the desire to conceal their homosexuality, attempting to test the "goodness of fit" of a heterosexual lifestyle, having a genuine affection for the female spouse, yielding to social pressures to adopt a conventional heterosexual lifestyle, escaping from homophobic feelings through marriage, escaping from a fear of loneliness, and having a desire for children (Bozett, 1981a; Fadiman, 1983).

THE PROBLEM

The research reported here constitutes an examination of factors that may motivate gay men to become parents, and to explore whether gay fathers may differ from heterosexual fathers regarding the value of children in their life as an adult.

METHOD

Sample

The sample consisted of 66 Caucasian men who were fathers of at least two children. Thirty-three of these men were self-identified homosexuals who were members of an organized support group for gay fathers in Denver, Colorado. The remaining 33 (presumed heterosexual) men were selected by random computer analysis from a subject pool of respondents ($n = 1,700$) who had participated in an earlier research project conducted by the investigators. The mean age of the total sample was 40 years (range $= 26$ to 55 years). Of the 66 respondents, 6 were married, 48 were divorced, 8 were separated, and 4 had never been married. Mean level of income was $27,000 (range $= \$25,000$ to $34,000), and average education was high school graduate (range $= 12$ to 20 years of education). Each respondent was the father of at least two children who ranged in age from 3 to 24 years (mean age 11 years).

Procedure

The Value of Children (VOC) questionnaire was developed from a cross-national study by Arnold et al. (1975). This instrument is composed of 21 Likert-type scale items that address the positive values of children in adults' lives. Factor analysis of responses by Arnold et al. yielded six subscales from these items as reasons for having children: (a) Security-Continuity-Tradition, (b) Parental Satisfactions, (c) Role Motivations, (d) Happiness and Affection, (e) Goals and Incentives, and (f) Social Status. The men were asked to circle their responses to each of the 21 items on a 7-point scale ranging from strongly disagree to strongly agree. Reliability and validity data regarding this instrument are discussed by Arnold et al. Additional questionnaire items provided information about marital status, age, ethnic background, education, income, occupation, place of residence, religious affiliation, and number and age of children.

Cover letters and questionnaires were mailed to all members ($n = 68$) on the mailing list of a gay fathers' support group in Denver; 33 completed questionnaires were returned. Similar questionnaire packets were completed by 1,700 men as part of a larger research study, as noted previously, on the development of social competencies in children. These packets were voluntarily completed by various groups of persons attending conferences, workshops, and other large meetings related to parenting education. Computer analysis allowed for matching each gay father with a heterosexual father for age, marital status, level of income, ethnic background, and level of education. This matching process resulted in a sample of $n = 62$ heterosexual fathers from the larger group of $n = 1,700$. From this pool, a random sample of $n = 33$ was taken in order to match the gay fathers in sample size.

RESULTS

Standard t tests were used to compare responses of gay fathers with heterosexual fathers on each subscale as well as on each item of the VOC scale. These results are summarized in Table 1. Given the response range from 1 to 7 for each item, a mean of 4 indicates a neutral position, less than 4 indicates a negative response, and means greater than 4 indicate positive reasons for wanting children.

Statistically significant differences between gay and heterosexual fathers were found with responses to two of the six subscales: (a) Tradition-Continuity-Security ($t = .73, df = 64, p < .05$); and (b) Social Status ($t = 4.08, df = 64, p < .01$). No significant differences were found between the two groups on the Parenthood Satisfactions, Role Motivations, Happiness and Affection, and Goals and Incentives subscales.

Analysis of responses by gay and heterosexual fathers to the individual items of the VOC scale produced significant differences on 5 of the 21 items.

Table 1.

ITEM ANALYSIS OF THE VOC SCALE: GAY VS. HETEROSEXUAL FATHERS

Item	Gay Father Mean	SD	Heterosexual Father Mean	SD	t	p
Security, Continuity, Traditional Subscale	2.74	.84	2.93	1.19	.73	.05
1. After becoming a parent, a person is less likely to behave immorally.	1.94	1.54	3.03	1.81	2.64	.01
Role Motivation Subscale					ns	
2. A boy becomes a man only after he is a father.	2.15	1.52	1.49	.80	2.23	.05
Goals and Incentives Subscale					ns	
3. Having children makes a stronger bond between husband and wife.	3.15	2.11	4.64	1.83	3.05	.001
Social Status Subscale	1.94	1.44	1.73	.92	4.08	.001
4. A young couple is not fully accepted into the community until they have children.	2.52	1.46	1.73	1.13	2.45	.01
5. A person with children is looked up to in the community more than a person without children.	3.36	1.95	1.73	1.04	4.25	.001

Parental Similarities

Results indicate that gay fathers generally are similar to heterosexual fathers in their reasons for having children. On the Social Status subscale, for instance, gay fathers, while disagreeing with these items as valid reasons for having children, disagreed significantly less than heterosexual fathers. However, there was greater variation among gay fathers in responding to these items as compared to the heterosexual fathers.

Parental Differences

Differences between gay and heterosexual fathers on the Tradition and Social Status subscales suggest reasons how gay men become involved in an event thought to be heterosexual in nature. Many fathers who later identify as being gay do so only after years of living a heterosexual lifestyle. These men marry, explore an intimate relationship with a woman, produce children, and adopt a variety of attitudes and behaviors that represent a heterosexual orientation. Many report maintaining or experimenting with their homosexual interests, although these are usually approached in a clandestine manner throughout the course of the marriage (Bozett, 1981a, 1985). The man who is gay but also a father may differ from other gay men by internalizing the negative cultural image of homosexuals and homosexuality and "protecting" himself from disapproval or rejection by significant others in his life and by society in general by marrying and becoming a parent. On the other hand, many gay men, despite their knowledge and acceptance of homosexual feelings, may adopt marriage and parenthood as a valuable and viable way of life because they truly desire children and value the role children play in their lives.

Item Analysis

The item analysis results indicate more specifically how gay men who are fathers perceive the role of children in their lives. Gay fathers do not accept the notion that children improve a marriage to the same degree as the heterosexual fathers. Gay fathers also do not believe to the degree the heterosexual fathers do that children function to enhance the morality of one's behavior. However, gay fathers tend to agree more than their heterosexual counterparts that the production of children enhances one's masculinity and that parenthood provides an entrance into the adult community, as well as to being accepted by other adults in the heterosexual community.

Overall, however, both groups of fathers tend to hold negative attitudes about children and child rearing (i.e., their mean scores on the 21 VOC items are less than 4). This finding is related to the socioeconomic status of the respondents. As Miller, Jacobsen, and Bigner (1981) have shown, individuals coming from urban residences who have a high level of income and education tend to respond negatively to the items on this questionnaire. Several researchers note that upper-middle-class persons give higher priority to self-actualization than to children and child rearing (Miller, Bigner, Jacobsen, & Turner, 1982; Miller et al., 1981). Gay fathers do not appear to be significantly different from heterosexual fathers in this regard.

Summary

To summarize the findings discussed above, we find that the two father groups did not differ significantly on the VOC scale. However, two subscales revealed statistically significant differences. In regards to Tradition-Continuity-Security, gay fathers' marriages and family orientations reflect not only a traditional attitude toward family life, but can also serve to protect against societal rejection. Similarly, for Social Status, having and valuing a child may indicate a sincere desire to attain some type of social status in one's community. Finally, both father groups tend to value children negatively, a finding previously identified for well-educated, high income, urban residents.

How representative our sample of gay fathers is is unknown. Many gay fathers remain in marriages, and others do not live an openly gay lifestyle. Moreover, both the gay and heterosexual samples here were limited to white, urban, upper-middle-class fathers. The gay fathers who composed the group in this study also may be considered select as they were members of a gay fathers support group. It is possible that their responses reflect attitudes not held by gay fathers who are not involved in such groups. Moreover, the heterosexual orientation of the comparison father group was merely inferred.

Despite these difficulties, our findings suggest that parenthood is experienced for similar reasons by both gay and heterosexual men. The findings await replication with better controlled and more diverse samples.

REFERENCES

Arnold, F., Culatao, R., Buripakdi, C., Chung, F., Fawcett, J., Iritani, T., Lee, S., & Wu, T. (1975). *The value of children* (Vol. 1). Honolulu: University of Hawaii Press.

Bell, A. P., & Weinberg, M. S. (1978). *Homosexualities: A study of diversity among men and women*. New York: Simon & Schuster.

Bozett, F. (1980). Gay fathers: How and why they disclose their homosexuality to their children. *Family Relations, 29*, 173-179.

Bozett, F. W. (1981a). Gay fathers: Evolution of the gay father identity. *American Journal of Orthopsychiatry, 51*, 552-559.

Bozett, F. W. (1981b). Gay fathers: Identity conflict resolution through integrative sanctioning. *Alternative Lifestyles, 4*, 90-107.

Bozett, F. W. (1985). Gay men as fathers. In S. Hansen & F. W. Bozett (Eds.), *Dimensions of fatherhood* (pp. 327-352). Beverly Hills, CA: Sage Publications.

Clark, D. (1979). Being a gay father. In B. Berzon & R. Leighton (Eds.), *Positively gay* (pp. 112-122). Millbrae, CA: Celestial Arts.

Fadiman, A. (1983, May). The double closet. *Life Magazine*, pp. 76-100.

Gibbs, J., & Martin, W. (1964). *Status integration and suicide: A sociological study*. Eugene, OR: University of Oregon Press.

Harris, M. B., & Turner, P. H. (1985-1986). Gay and lesbian parents. *Journal of Homosexuality, 12*(2), 101-113.

Maddox, B. (1982, February). Homosexual parents. *Psychology Today*, pp. 62-69.

Miller, B. (1979). Gay fathers and their children. *The Family Coordinator, 28*, 544-552.

Miller, J., Jacobsen, R. B., & Bigner, J. (1981). Liberal arts versus vocational college students and the value of children. *Journal of College Student Personnel, 22*, 436-439.

Miller, J., Bigner, J., Jacobsen, R. B., & Turner, J. (1982). The value of children for farm families: A comparison of mothers and fathers. In N. Stinnett (Ed.), *Family strengths 4: Positive support systems* (pp. 33-42). Lincoln, NE: University of Nebraska Press.

Robinson, B., & Skeen, P. (1982). Sex-role orientation of gay fathers versus gay non-fathers. *Perceptual and Motor Skills, 55*, 1055-1059.

Voeller, B., & Walters, J. (1978). Gay fathers. *The Family Coordinator, 27*, 149-157.

Weinberg, M. S., & Williams, C. J. (1974). *Male homosexuals: Their problems and adaptations*. New York: Penguin.

Parenting Behaviors of Homosexual and Heterosexual Fathers

Jerry J. Bigner, PhD
R. Brooke Jacobsen, PhD

Colorado State University

SUMMARY. Responses of 33 homosexual (gay) fathers were compared with those of 33 heterosexual (nongay) fathers on the Iowa Parent Behavior Inventory, an empirical measure of dimensions of parenting behavior. Gay fathers did not differ significantly from nongay fathers in their reported degree of involvement nor in intimacy level with children. Gay fathers tended to be more strict, more responsive to children's needs, and to provide reasons for appropriate behavior to children more consistently than nongay fathers. Several explanations are explored for these similarities and differences in parenting styles.

Within the past two decades, the existence of the homosexual subculture has been widely acknowledged by the nongay population. The term "subculture" is appropriate in that a value system has been defined by homosexuals that promotes an appropriate and satisfying lifestyle. Evidence for this value system can be found in several ways. For example, there are newsletters and newspapers among homosexual communities, support groups that assist individuals in making successful adjustments to gay lifestyles, and networking that is available through health clubs, social groups, and so on. Hence, the gradual emergence of the homosexual subculture has led to an increasing interest in and understanding of its inner

---

Correspondence and requests for reprints may be addressed to the authors at the Department of Human Development and Family Studies, Colorado State University, Ft. Collins, CO 80523.

173

workings and organization. Research has been accumulating slowly about this neglected portion of our society.

A SUBCULTURE WITHIN A SUBCULTURE

Gay fathers, or more specifically the subgroup of homosexual men who are also fathers, is becoming the focus of an increasing amount of research attention. Information about these fathers and their parenting styles is very limited. Partially responsible for this is the relatively small number of gay fathers. It is impossible to gain an accurate estimate because many of these men maintain a marriage relationship with a woman. Researchers propose, however, that approximately 20 to 25% of self-identified gay men also are fathers (Bell & Weinberg, 1978; Maddox, 1982; Miller, 1979; Weinberg & Williams, 1974). Another factor that accounts for the restricted research information is that a gay father is socioculturally unique. He wishes to act in two apparently opposing roles: that of a father (with all its usual connotations) and that of a homosexual man.

The lifestyle of the contemporary gay father presents a contradiction because being a parent is a highly valued status in our society. Most adults eventually become parents (U.S. Bureau of the Census, 1987), and actively participate within this role by being involved in children's lives. At the same time, this person maintains an identity as a homosexual. Hence, he is placed in a dynamic conflict.

At another level, the gay father is faced with yet another dilemma: the fact that his occupational role may be his primary focus and the fathering role itself may be a secondary role (LeMasters, 1974). Most likely, despite many social pressures, this is still the case for many men today. Despite the ever increasing numbers of dual-occupation families, mothers continue to retain the primary parenting responsibility (Lamanna & Riedman, 1988).

The Gay Father: A Role Under Pressure

It should be seen that the role of a gay father is filled with contradictions that are imposed both externally and internally. At the societal level, his role as a father is viewed as secondary; that is, he is perceived as not well prepared to parent children and as strongly attracted to and preoccupied with his occupational role. Evidence for this can be observed in the decades-old legal precedent of assigning child *support* to the father and child *custody* to the mother in the case of a divorce. The courts have ruled consistently in this manner, and these rulings are simply a reinforcement of the father-role-as-secondary stereotype for men in our society.

At the personal level, this renders an even more difficult situation for the gay father. Here, the negative stereotype about fathers in general may change into a bias giving the gay father not one but two strikes against him. He may be perceived almost as a social pariah because of the assumption that he may do irreparable harm to his children because of his sexuality. Thus, his institutional and personal sources of support are weakened, society and the legal systems reject him, and his nongay acquaintances also may reject him.

Finally, the homosexual subculture itself may not completely accept him due to his commitment and involvement in parental responsibilities (Bozett, 1987). Thus, the gay father is both structurally and psychologically at social odds with his interest in keeping one foot in both worlds: parenting and homosexuality.

Perhaps the most important factor about the negative stereotyping of a gay father is that very few empirically based studies have been conducted that measure actual parenting behaviors, styles, and activities. This limited research is discussed below, and we make the point that the stereotyping has been performed, as is usually the case, in the absence of empirical data. By this, we mean studies that show: (a) as a father, he relegates parenting to a secondary place in his life (societal stereotype); and (b) as a gay father he is a parent who creates disharmony, disorganization, and maladjustment for a child's development. Furthermore, to our knowledge, few empirical studies have been conducted that make an explicit comparison of the parenting behaviors of gay versus nongay fathers. Such a comparative study would shed important light on the *assumed* dual dilemmas a gay father experiences: as a father he is not doing well, and as a gay father, he is doing even worse. This type of research would reveal the similarities and differences between the gay and nongay father. This research would be further enhanced if comparisons were made using data from a standard data collection instrument such as the Iowa Parent Behavior Inventory (Crase, Clark, & Pease, 1978). Results, hence, can be compared generally with other studies that have used this instrument.

Is the Gay Father Stereotype Based in Fact?

The research reported below focuses upon the problem of collecting a set of data measuring the parenting behaviors of gay fathers. If the negative stereotype is based in fact, this needs to be known; conversely, if the stereotype has no empirical roots, this also needs to be known. In either case, this subculture within a subculture will be better understood.

Research on Gay Fathering

Few studies have examined the parenting behaviors of gay fathers (Harris & Turner, 1986; Miller, 1979; Riddle, 1978; Scallen, 1982). The consensus of these studies suggests that homosexuality is not incompatible with effective parenting. No differences can be found between nongay and gay fathers in problem solving, providing recreation for children, encouraging autonomy, handling problems relating to child rearing, having relatively few serious problems with children, and having generally positive relationships with children (Harris & Turner, 1986; Miller, 1979; Scallen, 1982). Gay fathers are reported to have greater satisfaction with their first child, fewer disagreements with partners over discipline, and a greater tendency to encourage play with sex-typed toys (e.g., those that are clearly intended for boys or girls only) (Harris & Turner, 1986).

In addition, publicly identified gay fathers, in comparison to the more "closeted" gay fathers who are still married, have been found to be less authoritative, use less corporal punishment, and experience stronger desires to rear children with nonsexist, egalitarian standards (Miller, 1979). These findings are important in helping to resolve child custody issues, especially when judges make rulings that are "in the best interests" of the child. Such rulings frequently are influenced by myths that children who have a gay parent also may grow up to be gay or that they may be sexually molested by the parent's gay friends and partners (Hall, 1978).

Methodological problems exist in each of these studies in that sampling problems as well as measurement difficulties are evident. The Scallen study used self-reports from a convenience sample of gay and nongay fathers who participated in father support groups. The Miller study used interview data from a representative sample of gay fathers but addressed issues other than child rearing concerns as the major focus of the study. The Harris and Turner study, while using empirical data from questionnaires, had serious sampling difficulties. It has extremely small groups of gay ($n = 10$) and nongay fathers ($n = 2$) as its sample. The validity and reliability of measurement devices used in this study can be questioned as well because no data are reported for these constructs as the instruments were custom designed for this particular study.

The Problem

The focus of this study, then, was on providing empirically based data on parenting behaviors of self-identified gay and nongay men by using a standardized instrument designed for this purpose. The research question that this study addressed was: Are there specific dimensions of parenting behavior that differentiate gay from nongay fathers?

METHOD

Subjects

The sample consisted of 66 men who were fathers of at least two children. Thirty-three of these men were self-identified homosexuals. Subjects composing this group were solicited from the mailing list of an organized support group for gay fathers in Denver, Colorado. The remaining 33 men, who were presumed to be nongay, were selected by random computer analysis from a subject pool of respondents ($n = 1,700$) who had participated in a large Western regional research project conducted by the investigators between 1980 and 1985. These men were assumed to be nongay because there was no comparable way to identify sexual orientation as with the gay father group. The mean age of the total sample was 40 years; marital status included 6 who were married, 48 who were divorced, 8 who were separated, and 4 who were never married.

The mean income was $27,000. The mean level of education was high school graduate. All men in the sample were white. Each subject was the father of at least two children, and the mean age of the children was 11 years.

Testing Material and Procedure

The Iowa Parent Behavior Inventory

The Iowa Parent Behavior Inventory (Crase et al., 1978) was completed by all subjects. This scale is composed of 36 Likert-type items composed of five factors or dimensions of parenting behavior. These include (a) *involvement with children*: the degree of active involvement with children such as playing with the child, physically helping the child with tasks, and facilitation of children's problem solving; (b) *limit-setting*: the degree of consistency in setting and enforcing rules and regulations for appropriate child behavior and the extent to which daily routines are defined; (c) *responsiveness*: the degree to which a parent responds promptly to a child's expressions of need, regardless of the immediacy of the expressed need; (d) *reasoning guidance*: the degree to which the parent reasons with a child to help him or her learn acceptable behavior and the degree to which the parent is supportive of the child's emotional expression; (e) *intimacy*: the degree to which the parent is open in his expression of physical affection to the child. The following data is provided by Crase et al. (1978) regarding each factor: (a) parental involvement is composed of seven items with a total variance of .84; (b) limit-setting is composed of nine items with a total variance of .82; (c) responsiveness is composed of seven items with a total variance of .81; (d) reasoning guidance is composed of 10 items with a total variance of .86; and (e) intimacy is composed of three items with a total variance of .64.

Scoring

Each item on the Inventory requires a Likert-type rating from 1 to 5 to indicate the degree of agreement or disagreement with each statement. Responses included (a) "I almost never behave this way"; (b) "I seldom behave this way"; (c) " I behave this way

about half the time or I'm not sure how often I behave this way";
(d) "I often behave this way"; or (e) "I almost always behave this
way." Thus, a 1 indicates a low score, and a 5 indicates a high
score for the characteristic described by each item. The weighted
score for each item in each factor is totaled, and the total score is
used for analysis of the data. As this is an instrument designed for
research rather than diagnostic purposes, a cumulative or total score
is irrelevant other than for data analysis.

Data Collection

This instrument, in addition to a cover letter and items requesting
demographic information, was mailed to all members on the mailing list of a gay fathers support group in Denver. A total of 68
questionnaire packets were mailed, and a total of 33 were returned
to the investigators. Similar questionnaire packets were completed
by a larger number of respondents as part of a larger study on the
development of social competencies in children, as noted above.
This packet was completed by various groups of individuals during
their attendance at conferences, workshops, and other large meetings that related to parenting education. These were completed on a
voluntary basis by each respondent and collected following their
completion by the investigators or their assistants. Computer analysis allowed for matching each gay father with a nongay father subject on age, marital status, level of income, ethnic background, and
level of education. This matching process resulted in a sample of n
$= 62$ nongay fathers from the larger group of $n = 1,700$. From this
pool a random sample of $n = 33$ was taken in order to match the
gay fathers in sample size.

We realize that the two father groups were obtained under different conditions. We are well aware that a completely valid comparison of the two groups requires that (a) data gathered from both
groups be under similar conditions; and (b) an outside, or objective
measure should confirm the self-reported data. However, ours is an
initial, exploratory study, and the target group's (gay fathers) lifestyle may preclude data collection under ideal conditions. Little research has been conducted to date regarding gay fathers' parenting
behaviors. Yet this parental subgroup, and more generally, the gay

lifestyle, is an emergent variation of traditional family life. Given these restrictions upon the data collection process itself, we hope that the analysis discussed below will shed some light on, or at least open an avenue of research into, this unknown family arena.

FINDINGS

Two-tailed t tests were computed in order to compare responses of the two groups of fathers on each factor as a whole and on each item that composed each factor. The findings relating to each factor are presented first, followed by those items that were found to discriminate between the groups.

Of the five factors or dimensions of parenting behavior measured on the Iowa Inventory, three were found to discriminate significantly between gay and nongay fathers. These were: (a) limit setting ($t = 2.73$, $df = 64$, $p < .01$); (b) responsiveness ($t = 2.24$, $df = 64$, $p < .05$); and (c) reasoning guidance ($t = 2.42$, $df = 64$, $p < .01$). No differences were found between the two groups on factors of involvement or intimacy.

Analysis of responses between gay and nongay fathers on each item of the Inventory produced significant differences on 13 of the 36 items. This analysis was performed to provide additional information on specific behaviors within each factor. A synopsis of this analysis is shown in Table 1.

These results indicate that gay fathers tend to be more strict and consistently emphasize the importance of setting and enforcing limits on children's behavior significantly more as a group than nongay fathers. Additionally, gay fathers state that they go to greater lengths than nongay fathers in promoting cognitive skills of children by explaining rules and regulations to children. As such, they may place greater emphasis on verbal communications with children as compared with nongay fathers. Gay fathers tend to be more responsive to the perceived needs of children than nongay fathers.

Although no differences can be found on two of the factors (involvement and intimacy) as a whole due to small variances in responses, significant differences were found on individual items of the involvement and intimacy factors. Differences in responses between the two groups suggest that gay fathers tend to go to extra lengths to act as a resource for activities with children when compared with nongay fathers. Whereas gay fathers were no different from nongay fathers on the intimacy factor, one item was particularly significant in discriminating between these groups. This item referred to demonstrations of affection between the father and his partner in the child's presence. Gay fathers indicated that they were less willing to be demonstrative than were nongay fathers.

Item analysis on the reasoning and guidance factor showed that gay fathers were more egalitarian than nongay fathers. This is shown by the differences in responses on the item measuring the child's participation in family decisions. Gay fathers also were much more likely to act in a counselor role than nongay fathers. They reportedly encouraged children to discuss their fears with them more frequently than the nongay fathers.

In general, however, it may be concluded that gay fathers are similar to nongay fathers in their overall parenting abilities and skills. They are significantly different from gay fathers, however, in their approach, philosophy, and style of parenting.

DISCUSSION

Several explanations can be suggested that address the differences and similarities in parenting behavior of gay and nongay fathers. First, gay fathers may feel additional pressures to be more proficient at their parenting role than nongay fathers. Factors that might motivate them to want to be "better" fathers could include: (a) stronger feelings of guilt about their role in fathering children, based on an increased sensitivity about their sexuality; or (b) sensitivity to the belief that they are "on the spot" or expected to perform better due to a fear that visitation or custody decisions could be challenged because of their sexual preference. This can be illustrated by the differences in responses on the limit-setting factor.

Gay fathers tend to be more authoritative and to "run a tight ship" in the execution of their control over children. They may believe that they are being examined more closely than other fathers due to their sexual preference and the challenges that this close examination presents to their fathering abilities.

Second, the findings suggest that gay fathers may be more an-

Table 1
Item Analysis of Responses on the Iowa Parent Behavior Inventory: Gay Versus Nongay Fathers

Item	Gay Father Mean	Nongay Father Mean	$\underline{t}$	$\underline{p}$
Parental involvement factor				
Find children's books, reference books, or records that you and your child can share together.	3.5	3.0	2.18	.05
Help your child select items that interest him or her at the store.	3.7	2.6	4.14	.001
Find crafts such as painting, coloring, woodworking, or needlework you and your child can do together on cold rainy days.	3.0	4.1	4.55	.001
Suggest to your child indoor games that you and she or he might play together.	3.4	2.6	3.33	.001
Limit setting factor				
Require your child to remain seated in the car while you are driving.	4.5	2.3	9.33	.001
Enforce rules for your child concerning pushing or shoving of other children.	3.6	4.3	2.55	.01
Maintain the limits you set for your child's behavior in public places like basketball games, church, or grocery stores.	4.0	3.3	2.52	.01
Require your child to put away his or her clothes.	3.3	2.7	2.26	.05

Responsiveness factor				
Give your child things he or she especially likes when he or she is ill.	3.7	4.4	2.73	.01
Go immediately to your child when you see him or her hurt from a fall off a bicycle.	4.1	2.9	4.02	.001
Reasoning guidance factor				
Talk with your child about his or her fears of the dark, of animals, or of school failures.	4.4	2.9	5.89	.001
Ask your child for his or her opinion in family decisions.	4.2	3.4	3.13	.01
Intimacy factor				
Hug or kiss your spouse in the presence of your child.	3.4	4.3	2.53	.01

drogynous than nongay fathers in their parenting orientation. As such, they may incorporate a greater degree and combination of expressive role functions than the more traditionally sex-role oriented nongay fathers. These expressive role functions are seen more conventionally in the female, mothering role. This is suggested by the differences in responses of the two groups on the responsiveness and reasoning guidance factors. It can be inferred that gay fathers in this study are less likely than nongay fathers to conduct their parenting style in the conventional male sex-role related fashion. The cultural image or stereotype of the father role is that adult males (a) generally are not interested in children or child rearing issues (b) view the occupational role as the primary parenting identity (c) are less competent caregivers than women and (d) are less nurturant than women toward children (Bigner, 1985). It is possible that the nongay fathers most likely adopt this as their parenting style, and gay fathers *may* demonstrate a blending of the qualities traditionally associated with both mother and father role images.

Third, the similarities in responses on the involvement and intimacy factors and on the majority of items of the Inventory lend support to the notion that sexual orientation has no direct or deleterious effect on the gay father's ability to parent in an effective manner. This supports the findings of other researchers on this issue (Bozett, 1985; Harris & Turner, 1986; Miller, 1979; Robinson & Skeen, 1982). This is an important empirical finding that has bearing on custody and other legal decisions relating to the welfare of children who have a gay father.

Some caution should be exercised in generalizing the results of this study to the general population due to sampling difficulties that could not be avoided. This sample of gay fathers is unlikely to be an accurate representation of gay fathers in the general population. It is perhaps impossible to know just what is an accurate representation of this group because many gay fathers remain in marriages and others do not live an openly gay lifestyle. Several aspects of the men in this study also tend to bias this group of gay fathers as a representative sample. This sample was all white in composition, had a high level of income, and came from an urban area. Certainly, this is not typical or representative of gay fathers in the general population. The gay fathers who composed the group in this study also may be considered a select group as they were members of a gay fathers support group. It is possible that their responses reflect a distorted enthusiasm for children and child rearing in over-emphasizing the positive aspects of child rearing and parenting. Furthermore, it should be pointed out that the sexual orientation of the nongay fathers group was inferred because there was no way to confirm this at the time that they completed the survey material.

Despite these difficulties, it remains clear that gay fathers differ from nongay fathers in their degree of limit-setting, responsiveness, and reasoning guidance with children, but are similar to nongay fathers in involvement and intimacy with children. It is therefore possible to conclude that sexual preference of fathers produces qualitative differences in self-reported parenting behavior.

REFERENCES

Bell, A. P., & Weinberg, M. S. (1978). *Homosexualities: A study of diversity among men and women*. New York: Simon & Schuster.

Bigner, J. J. (1985). *Parent-child relations: An introduction to parenting* (2nd ed.). New York: Macmillan.

Bozett, F. (1985). Gay men as fathers. In S. Hanson & F. Bozett (Eds.), *Dimensions of fatherhood* (pp. 327-352). Beverly Hills, CA: Sage Publications.

Bozett, F. (1987). Gay fathers. In F. Bozett (Ed.), *Gay and lesbian parents* (pp. 3-22). New York: Praeger.

Crase, S., Clark, S., & Pease, D. (1978). *Iowa parent behavior inventory manual*. Ames, IA: Iowa State University Research Foundation.

Hall, M. (1978). Lesbian families: Cultural and clinical issues. *Social Work, 25,* 380-385.

Harris, M. B., & Turner, P. H. (1986). Gay and lesbian parents. *Journal of Homosexuality, 12*(2), 101-113.

Lamanna, M. A., & Reidman, A. (1988). *Marriages and families: Making choices and facing change* (3rd ed.). Belmont, CA: Wadsworth.

LeMasters, E. E. (1974). *Parents in modern America* (rev. ed.). Homework, IL: Dorsey.

Maddox, B. (1982, February). Homosexual parents. *Psychology Today*, pp. 62-69.

Miller, B. (1979). Gay fathers and their children. *The Family Coordinator, 28,* 544-552.

Riddle, D. (1978). Relating to children: Gays as role models. *Journal of Social Issues, 34,* 38-58.

Robinson, B., & Skeen, P. (1982). Sex-role orientation of gay fathers versus gay nonfathers. *Perceptual and Motor Skills, 55,* 1055-1059.

Scallen, A. (1982). An investigation of paternal attitudes and behavior in homo-sexual and nongay fathers. *Dissertation Abstracts International, 42*, 3809B.

U. S. Bureau of the Census. (1987). *Statistical abstract of the United States: 1986*. Washington, DC: U. S. Government Printing Office.

Weinberg, M., & Williams, C. (1974). *Male homosexuals: Their problems and adaptations*. New York: Oxford University Press.

BOOK REVIEWS

Robert J. Kus, RN, PhD

THE "SISSY BOY SYNDROME" AND THE DEVELOPMENT
OF HOMOSEXUALITY. Richard Green. *New Haven, CT, Yale
University Press, 1987.*

*The "Sissy Boy Syndrome" and the Development of Homosexu-
ality* is the culmination of an impressive amount of research, time,
and commitment.

Richard Green's book is an illumination on the type of boy
known as the "sissy." It examines his development, the role played
by his parents in his development, and his sexuality in adulthood.
The researcher interviewed sissy boys and their parents, and a control group of traditional boys and their parents.

The author is Professor of Psychiatry at the University of California, Los Angeles and directs the Program in Psychiatry, Law, and
Human Sexuality. He is also the founder of the *Archives of Sexual
Behavior* and the founding president of the International Academy
of Sex Research.

The book is well written and the language is lucid. The author
describes the methodology in detail and with enough clarity for a
sophisticated reader to evaluate easily the work itself and the appropriateness of its conclusions. Results are presented in a straightfor-

ward way, and the potentially dry material is presented in interesting slices of data, such as interviews. Finally, the author gives valuable admonishments to the reader not to misuse the data because it can be potentially dangerous to gay male children and to others.

Unfortunately, the book also contains some serious problems. First, the title is very misleading. From the subtitle, . . . *and the Development of Homosexuality,* "We would think that the book is about the development of homosexuality. This is not the case. The author tells us (p. 389) that "For a given 'feminine' boy, the answer to the question, 'Will this boy become [homosexual]?' must be answered, 'We don't know?'" Furthermore, the book is filled with discussions of nongay conditions as well as conditions that are rarely gay associated. Also, the author uses language that can be potentially dangerous. He does not see homosexuality as a lifelong, irreversible state of being that is recognized by gay males in their teen years. On the contrary, the author imagines that gay male children do not exist, but rather are neutral boys who may "become" gay. This is similar to the imagery of a cocoon that may, eventually, turn into a butterfly. Unfortunately, such a view of sexual orientation leads to a host of psychiatric and political barbarities. This suggests that if a gay person at one point in life is not gay, then it is possible to prevent him from becoming so if he can be identified at an early enough stage in his "nongay" state of being. Although Green cautions the reader not to use this data to harm others, he is naive to believe that this will be the case. He needs merely to look at the long history of efforts on the part of psychiatry and government to eliminate gay men through aversion techniques, psychoanalysis, and holocausts.

On a personal level, I found this book difficult to read and was uncertain about the rationale for the study. This model assumes that if we identify causes, then we can eliminate the undesirable characteristics. One wonders if, at least on a subconscious level, the author considers the idea of homosexuality as one of those "negative things." One's sexual orientation, like other nonchosen aspects of self, is a beautiful divine gift to be treasured and developed to its maximum.

This book is definitely not for the casual reader. Rather, it is for the well educated, highly sophisticated scholar in the field of gay studies. Further, the reader needs to have a strong historical perspective of the research methodology, and a strong sense of the uses and abuses of psychiatry and behavioral sciences toward gay men.

The book costs $40.00 and can be obtained from Yale University Press, 92A Yale Station, New Haven, CT 06520.

MAMA'S BOY. Bev Arthur and Martin Arthur. *San Francisco, Strawberry Hill Press, 1986.*

Mama's Boy is an autobiography of a mother (Bev Arthur) and gay son (Martin Arthur). It begins with the marriage of Bev to her first husband (Martin's father) and ends with her reflections on her young adult son's homosexuality.

The chapters are organized around time periods. A unique aspect of this book is that these time periods are examined from both mother's and son's perspectives in alternating chapters. For example, Bev tells of a time period in one chapter, and then Martin writes about that same time period in the following chapter.

Most of the book takes place in the State of Iowa where Martin grows up: from the small towns like Newton to the sophisticated university cities like Iowa City. The language Bev uses to describe the struggles of a family that is plagued by problems is beautiful, simple, and very moving. Martin describes and captures in his description the classic gay male childhood pattern, which I call "the best little boy in the world" syndrome, named after John Reid's autobiography of the same title. This pattern, common to the gay male's childhood, is characterized by a boy who is highly sensitive, loves to read, does well in school, and follows a "superachieving" path.

The book is well organized and the language is down-to-earth. With warmth and humor, two routine lives are portrayed in an extraordinary way, and where least expected, strength and inspiration emanate from a home that is racked with bereavement, alcoholism, job losses, and frequent moves.

I highly recommend *Mama's Boy* to all gay male teens and adults, parents and friends of gay men, men's studies scholars (especially those in the subspecialty of gay studies), and behavioral scientists interested in the growth and development of gay male children.

The book costs $9.95 and can be obtained from Strawberry Hill Press, 2594 15th Avenue, San Francisco, CA 94127.

DUAL IDENTITIES: COUNSELING CHEMICALLY DEPENDENT GAY MEN AND LESBIANS. Dana G. Finnegan and Emily B. McNally. *Center City, MN, Hazelden, 1987.*

Finally, a book for counselors that addresses alcoholism and related chemical dependencies, the number one health problem facing gay and lesbian adults in America today.

The book provides basic information on gay and lesbian clients for professionals who work with them in substance abuse treatment centers. In this work, "counselor" refers to all health professionals (nurses, social workers, physicians, and other therapists); "chemically dependent" refers to alcoholics and other chemically addicted individuals.

The book is divided into three sections. The first section addresses the basic life issues that are of prime concern to the gay and lesbian clients (i.e., internal and external homophobia). The second section deals with the coming out process and treatment information. The third section lists the resources for counselors to get additional information.

The authors, who are certified alcoholism counselors and work in this field, are eminently qualified to write this book. They are the founders of the National Association of Lesbian and Gay Alcoholism Professionals (NALGAP), an organization that is experiencing phenomenal growth, and they teach a three-week course at the Rutgers Summer School of Alcohol Studies.

Finnegan and McNally's book is the only book of its kind available. The book is geared primarily toward counselors who are heterosexual and who have little background in gay/lesbian issues. It captures the critical issues that need to be understood by chemical dependency counselors and is a valuable addition to any health professional who works with gay and lesbian substance abuse clients.

In addition to a solid bibliography, there's a helpful Suggested Readings List and an "organization audit" that is designed to help agencies look for evidence of homophobic and discrimination practices. The authors do an excellent job of treating the needs of both gay men and lesbian women equally. A "diagnosis of alcoholism and related chemical dependencies" test is included and can be used by any reader.

I recommend this easy-to-read book to all chemical dependency counselors who seek more information about the 10% of their clients who are gay and lesbian.

The book costs $7.95 and is available from Hazelden, Pleasant Valley Road, Box 176, Center City, MN 55012-0176.

COUNSELING OUR OWN: THE LESBIAN/GAY SUBCULTURE MEETS THE MENTAL HEALTH SYSTEM. Charna Klein. *Renton, WA, Publication Service, Inc., 1986.*

Counseling Our Own is an historical-political look at the gay and lesbian counseling movement from a lesbian-feminist perspective.

The author, Charna Klein, is trained as a psychological and medical anthropologist. She has worked at the Seattle Counseling Service for 7 years and has trained mental health professionals to look at the cultural diversity of their various clients.

In *Counseling Our Own*, Klein addresses the problems and the growth of gay and lesbian counseling centers. In her book, she examines, in-depth, the Seattle Counseling Services for Sexual Minorities, and several other agencies, though less intensely. She points out the various stages of development that gay and lesbian agencies have experienced since the late 1960s, and she looks at the types of clients they see and how they sought to meet the needs of gay and lesbian clients — needs often not met by mainstream mental health agencies. She shows us what happens when a nonmainstream agency begins to accept money from the taxpayers via the government.

Klein describes the staff of gay/lesbian agencies primarily in terms of their roles in political battles and in the kinds of political philosophies that they hold, rather than in terms of the special counseling skills that they bring to the therapeutic setting.

This book appeals to the well educated, scholarly reader, and not to the average gay or lesbian person on the street. In particular, it would be a valuable addition to: libraries of lesbian studies scholars; historians, sociologists, political scientists, and public policy makers interested in gay/lesbian issues; gay and lesbian counselors; students interested in a lesbian-feminist perspective of this aspect of post-Stonewall history; and lesbian-feminist oriented anthropologists and sociologists engaged in field work.

The strength of the book is its uniqueness, which in itself makes me recommend it. It has excellent appendices, which profile the clients and agencies studied, the research instruments used to gather the data, a reading and resource list, and a comprehensive bibliography.

The book is not without problems, and at times is somewhat rambling and disorganized. This fault, however, is forgivable, given that it is Klein's first book. Another problem, though more serious, is the antimale sexist rhetoric that may be offensive to gay and heterosexual men and to nonsexist women. For example, Klein makes statements such as "gay men being sexist" and ignores the antimale sexism that is rather rampant in the lesbian community. Despite this problem, the book's contributions outweigh the sexist rhetoric and justify my recommending it.

The book costs $11.49 (including postage and handling) and can be obtained from Consulting Services Northwest, Inc., 839 NE 96th Street, Seattle, WA 98115.

Afterword

This collection of articles attests to gay men and lesbians as members of families, either as children or as parents. Although this is not new information, Christian fundamentalists and conservative traditionalists persist in propagating the myth that gays and lesbians are antifamily. Moreover, social hostility is probably greater toward homosexuals than toward any other form of family. Gay and lesbian families are suppressed by legal, social, religious, and economic forces. The United States Supreme Court decision that upheld Georgia's antisodomy law, maintaining that the constitutional right to privacy does not extend to homosexual activity, is evidence. Moreover, the courts have removed children from their gay/lesbian parents solely because of parental homosexuality, not because of any deficiency on the part of the parents or the household. This is the case regardless of research findings that indicate that, "Children being raised by transsexual or homosexual parents do not differ appreciably from children raised in more conventional family settings on macroscopic measures of sexual identity" (Green, 1978). Furthermore, homosexual couples may not marry, and because of this are denied social security and insurance benefits, inheritance rights, and major medical care for live-in lovers. Gay men and lesbians are not protected under Title VII of the Civil Rights Act of 1964 because it does not include sexual orientation, and home ownership by unrelated individuals is illegal in some communities. Many other examples of the discrimination of homosexuals (legal and otherwise) could be provided.

However, in spite of this blatant prejudice, the gay/lesbian family is making some inroads as an authentic family form. Evidence of this can be found in several recent accounts. In the classic study *American Couples* (Blumstein & Schwartz, 1983), both gay male and lesbian couples were studied along with married and cohabiting heterosexual couples. In a lead article on factors that affect families

193

that appeared in *Report* (Rubin, 1987), an official publication of the National Council on Family Relations, a significant portion of the article dealt with issues related to the gay/lesbian family. Moreover, recent novels and autobiographical accounts have directly or indirectly addressed the topic. For example, in *The Lost Language of Cranes* by David Leavitt (1986), the gay protagonist has a gay father, and in *Good-bye, I Love You* (1986), Carol Lynn Pearson chronicles her life with her children and gay husband who dies from AIDS. Works such as these help to validate gays and lesbians further within the context of family. My own work, *Gay and Lesbian Parents* (Bozett, 1987), directly attested to the legitimacy of gays and lesbians against the background of both parents and family. All of these efforts are a part of the evolutionary process Miller refers to in the preface to this collection.

Rejection of the gay/lesbian family as a viable family form needs to be attacked on several fronts, not the least of which is through the legal system. Space does not allow for a full discussion of all the issues, so I will address only one for which I have special concern. Within the recent past states such as New Hampshire have made it illegal for gays to become foster or adoptive parents. In Florida, gays and lesbians have been prevented from adopting for many years. It is important that efforts be made to prevent or overturn such legislation. There is no evidence whatsoever that children reared in households in which one or both adults is homosexual are in any way at harm, either physically or psychologically. To deny children a loving and stable family environment solely because of the sexual orientation of the adult(s) in the household is without reason and unethical.

Moreover, children who themselves are gay and who need adoption or foster care would in all probability benefit immeasurably from being reared by a gay or lesbian parent or couple. Such parent(s) could assist these children's socialization into both the gay and nongay societies, thus helping these youngsters avoid the guilt and oftentimes almost unendurable pain that so many gay people have to overcome before they become productive, well-adjusted members of society. It would likely be of inestimable benefit to both the children and society as a whole for gay children to be reared by an adoptive or foster gay parent who could be a positive gay role model, who could assist the children's acculturation into the gay world, and who could also facilitate their adaptation and adjustment to the nongay world. To deny gay men and lesbians the right to adopt or to become foster parents is inhumane, and an incredible waste of human potential. Similar arguments are extant for biological gay/lesbian parents; their right to parent their own children should never be denied except on legitimate grounds, and certainly never solely on the basis of their sexual orientation.

Much research is needed in order to establish the gay/lesbian family as an appropriate form of family in which to rear children. For example, on the basis of the above discussion, objective evidence of the effect of gay/lesbian adoptive/foster parenting on gay/lesbian youth is needed in order to counteract legislation or policy that prohibits it. Moreover, both cross-sectional and longitudinal study of gay/lesbian families is needed to determine what effects parental homosexuality has on children beyond the pre-oedipal and oedipal phases of development and into their adulthood. It is also important to identify the unique strengths of these families, as well as strengths that are similar to nongay families, in addition to discovering their lifestyle stages and developmental tasks so that the "typical" or "normal" gay/lesbian family can be described and understood. Research is also needed to ascertain the range of "normal" gay/lesbian parenting styles and behaviors, and to ascertain determinants of the "healthy" gay/lesbian family, so that atypical behaviors and family pathologies can be identified. It will be impossible to provide gay/lesbian families with counseling that has a substantial scientific foundation until the differences between the healthy and disordered can be discerned.

Lastly, the gay/lesbian family as a substantive content area needs to be incorporated in gay studies curricula, and it needs to become a domain of interest in the field of family science. Likewise, researchers, educators, and practitioners, both gay and nongay, need to become sensitized to the notion of the gay family in its multiple forms, so that regardless of how these families are constituted, they become understood and treated by the legal, health care, religious, and other institutions of society with the same sensitivity and respect accorded nongay families.

Frederick W. Bozett, RN, DNS

REFERENCES

Blumstein, P., & Schwartz, P. (1983). *American couples*. New York: William Morrow.

Bozett, F. W. (1987). *Gay and lesbian parents*. New York: Praeger.

Green, R. (1978). Sexual identity of 37 children raised by homosexual or transsexual parents. *American Journal of Psychiatry, 135*, 692-697.

Leavitt, D. (1986). *The lost language of cranes*. New York: Knopf.

Miller, B. (1989). Preface. *Journal of Homosexuality, 17*(3/4), xi-xiv.

Pearson, C. L. (1986). *Good-bye, I love you*. New York: Random House.

Rubin, R. H. (1987). Many factors affect families. *National Council on Family Relations Report, 32*(2), 1.

Index